Other Kaplan Success with Words Books

Success with American Idioms
Success with Legal Words
Success with Medical Words
Success with Words for the TOEFL

Related Kaplan Books

Access America's Guide to Studying in the U.S.A.
Kaplan/Newsweek Business School Admissions Adviser
Kaplan/Newsweek Graduate School Admissions Adviser
TOEFL
TOEIC

Success with
Business Words

By Lin Lougheed and the
Staff of Kaplan Educational Centers

Simon & Schuster

Kaplan Books
Published by Kaplan Educational Centers and Simon & Schuster
1230 Avenue of the Americas
New York, NY 10020

Project Editor: Julie Schmidt
Cover Design: Cheung Tai
Interior Page Design: Michael Shevlin
Production Editor: Maude Spekes
Desktop Publishing Manager: Michael Shevlin
Managing Editor: Brent Gallenberger
Executive Editor: Del Franz
Executive Director, International Products and Programs:
Marilyn J. Rymniak

Special thanks to Amy Arner Sgarro, Enid Burns, and Pamela Vittorio

Manufactured in the United States of America
Published simultaneously in Canada

July 1998

10 9 8 7 6 5 4 3 2 1

Library of Congress Cataloging in Publication Data in progress

ISBN 0-684-85398-1

Table of Contents

How to Use This Book

If you've studied English, you know that after you've reached a certain level, you need to work on refining and improving your vocabulary. As you become more familiar with the English language, you want to be able to use and understand the same sophisticated, professional business vocabulary as your American classmates or colleagues.

Success with Business Words is an invaluable tool for student or professional, nonnative speakers of English seeking to attend business school or to enter business-related professions in the United States. It uses a variety of methods to help you to incorporate 450 business words and phrases into your vocabulary. Certain phrases vary in meaning according to the context in which they are used, and may appear in more than one chapter.

Each of the 30 chapters in this book focuses on words or phrases that are related to a particular theme, such as *Accounting* or *Investment*. Each chapter offers three different types of exercises that encourage you to contextualize and actively use these words or phrases. The first exercise consists of two columns in which 15 words or phrases listed in the left-hand column are to be matched with the correct definitions in the right-hand column. You should try to see how many phrases and meanings you can match up without using your dictionary. If this proves difficult, move on to the passages on the second page of the chapter and try reading them aloud to yourself or with a partner. The two conversations and the short talk you will find here use the terms from the matching list in relevant, realistic contexts. Seeing these phrases in their proper context should enable you to go back to the first exercise and match any terms that you were not able to figure out earlier with their meanings.

On the third page of each chapter, there is a fill-in-the-blank exercise that tests your understanding of the 15 words and expressions covered in the chapter. In this exercise you will "recycle" your vocabulary by putting the phrases that you learned in the matching exercise and passages into sentences, contextualizing them further. This will aid you in retaining them as "learned" vocabulary. Be aware that these exercises occasionally ask you to provide the term in a different part of speech or tense than that which is used in the matching list. This encourages you to develop and reinforce a sense of how the term is actively used in everyday business English.

After you have completed the fill-in-the-blank exercise, you should review your work and check your answers in the answer keys on the fourth and final page of each chapter. Then read the conversations and short talk one more time to check your comprehension again.

You may work through these chapters in sequence, or by topic of interest. You can also look up unfamiliar words and phrases in the index and do the exercises that center around them. Whichever method you choose, you will master commonly used business terms relevant to your chosen field of interest.

Good luck and enjoy using this book!

1 Accounting

Match each word or phrase to its meaning:

1. to reconcile	to have income exactly equal to costs
2. ledger	an amount or value expressed in numbers
3. fiscal	worksheet
4. to break even	nearly exact; more or less
5. to estimate	leader
6. figures	a given number of units divided by the total number of units
7. on average	following one another in uninterrupted order
8. spreadsheet	the amount by which a sum falls short of the required amount
9. budget	an account book containing all business transactions
10. approximately	to drop the change and make the figure an even amount
11. to close out	to make an approximate calculation
12. head	a plan of expected income and expenses
13. consecutive	to dispose of finally and completely
14. deficit	to bring into agreement
15. to round off	pertaining to financial matters

Can you figure out the meaning of the italicized words in the following passages?

Conversation One:

RYAN: In going over the *ledger*, it appears we have a *deficit*.

ANN: That's impossible. We haven't overspent. Let me know when you *reconcile* the accounts.

RYAN: Oh, I see what happened. I made a mistake when I *rounded off* the numbers.

Conversation Two:

ANN: The accounting department announced that the company will finally *break even* this year.

RYAN: After three *consecutive* years of losses, that'd be a welcome change.

ANN: If sales continue to rise as they have been, they *estimate* that within the year, revenues will double.

RYAN: Let's just hope the economy stays strong and people keep spending.

Short Talk:

Our *fiscal* year ends in October, so we'll need to *close out* our books. This is also the time when the department *heads* need to come up with a budget for next year. Accounting has prepared a *spreadsheet* laying out *figures* to keep in mind when you're preparing your *budgets*. *On average*, each department spends *approximately* $2,000 a month on expenses, which must be itemized in your *budgets*.

KAPLAN

Fill in the blanks to complete the sentences:

16. It's wise to have a _____ so you can better plan how you spend your money.

17. All _____ matters are to be handled by the finance department.

18. _____, he spends three hours a week on the phone handling complaints.

19. She's been elected president of the board for two _____ terms.

20. Record each transaction in the _____ so we have an accurate record of our operating expenses.

21. A _____ is made up of columns containing data.

22. We need to _____ our books for this year, which means receipts and expense reports must be submitted so we can reconcile our accounts.

23. _____ one out of every five small businesses goes out of business each year.

24. Let's review the _____ to see if our numbers match.

25. Just drop off the cents and _____ to the nearest dollar.

26. The _____ will meet next month to discuss their committee's work.

27. If our revenue increases by four percent, we can pay all of our debts and _____.

28. I have to be better about balancing my checkbook; I can't seem to _____ the account to get my numbers to agree with my bank statement.

29. The construction will cost $10,000 and we allocated only $6,000 to it, which means we'll have a _____ of $4,000.

30. Can you _____ how much the new computer installation will cost?

Answer Key

1. to bring into agreement
2. an account book containing all business transactions
3. pertaining to financial matters
4. to have income exactly equal to costs
5. to make an approximate calculation
6. an amount or value expressed in numbers
7. a given number of units divided by the total number of units
8. worksheet
9. a plan of expected income and expenses
10. nearly exact; more or less
11. to dispose of finally and completely
12. leader
13. following one another in uninterrupted order
14. the amount by which a sum falls short of the required amount
15. to drop the change and make the figure an even amount

16. budget
17. fiscal
18. on average
19. consecutive
20. ledger
21. spreadsheet
22. close out
23. approximately
24. figures
25. round off
26. heads
27. break even
28. reconcile
29. deficit
30. estimate

2 | Banking

Match each word or phrase to its meaning:

1. statement   to change; to go up and down
2. deposit   spending more than available
3. withdrawal   to borrow money from the bank
4. to fluctuate   act of taking money out of account
5. installments   to borrow money from bank for purchase of home

6. reserve   money held aside for later use
7. credit   to combine into one
8. overdraft   money added to account
9. bounced   amount of money in account
10. balance   relationship with a bank in which it holds your money

11. to mortgage   series of partial payments
12. to take out a loan   record of business transactions
13. to consolidate   to make invalid
14. account   describes a check returned because there is not enough cash in account to cover it

15. void   money made available based on trust in one's ability to meet payments

Can you figure out the meanings of the italicized words in the following passages?

Conversation One:

MRS. JONES: Good morning. I need to make a *deposit* into my checking *account*.

HILARY: I see you have a negative *balance* and two checks have *bounced*. If you add *overdraft* protection to your *account*, you'll have a *reserve* of *credit* in case you overspend the cash in your *account*.

MRS. JONES: Thanks. I thought I had *voided* a check that was cashed, which is what caused the overdraft.

Conversation Two:

MRS. JONES: Interest rates are the lowest in years. Sam certainly chose the right time to buy a house and *take out* a *mortgage*.

MR. SMITH: Rates *fluctuate* so often, I can't keep up with them. I should pay more attention, because I want to *take out a loan* for a new car.

MRS. JONES: I have ten more *installments* to pay on my car.

Short Talk:

Electronic banking is the latest advancement in banking services. Using a computer, you can check your *account* activity and *balance* 24 hours a day. No more waiting in line at the bank. You will receive *consolidated* monthly bank *statements* that list all your *accounts* in one easy to understand document. You can make your *deposits* and *withdrawals*, pay your bills, and maintain your *account* online. Imagine the time and money you'll save in the convenience of your own home!

Fill in the blanks to complete the sentences:

16. Mike opened a savings _____ at the bank so he could save his money and earn interest instead of spending it frivolously.

17. _____ serve as documentation of your account balances, deposits, withdrawals, and other information.

18. His check _____ because he didn't have enough money in his checking account to cover the amount of the check he wrote.

19. I need to make a _____ from my account so we can have cash to spend tonight when we go out to dinner.

20. You can _____ your bills by transferring all your outstanding balances to one credit card.

21. Paying for a large purchase in monthly _____ makes it easier to afford.

22. A _____ is a loan that is borrowed from banks and other financial institutions to purchase a house.

23. Each time you make a _____ into your savings account, you increase the amount of interest you'll make on that money.

24. Interest rates _____ with the ups and downs in the economy.

25. Spending more than you have in your account will result in an _____ if you're not careful.

26. People usually _____ from the bank so they can buy things they can't afford to pay for all at once.

27. If you make a mistake when writing a check, just write _____ on it and the check will no longer be valid.

28. You might never use it, but setting aside a _____ of cash can be useful in case of an emergency.

29. Banks issue _____ to customers who they know can pay back the short-term money borrowed to make smaller purchases.

30. Your account _____ is the amount of money you have in the bank.

Answer Key

1. record of business transactions

2. money added to account

3. act of taking money out of account

4. to change; to go up and down

5. series of partial payments

6. money held aside for later use

7. money made available based on trust in one's ability to meet payments

8. spending more than available

9. describes a check returned because there is not enough cash in account to cover it

10. amount of money in account

11. to borrow money from bank for purchase of home

12. to borrow money from bank

13. to combine into one

14. relationship with a bank in which it holds your money

15. to make invalid

16. account

17. statements

18. bounced

19. withdrawal

20. consolidate

21. installments

22. mortgage

23. deposit

24. fluctuate

25. overdraft

26. take out a loan

27. void

28. reserve

29. credit

30. balance

3 Billing

Match each word or phrase to its meaning:

1. to acknowledge — goods that are bought and sold
2. grace period — history of behavior
3. billing cycle — to pay what you owe
4. invoice — proof of purchase or payment
5. receipt — to have things you will buy listed for payment all at once when you are finished buying
6. finance charges — to sign one's name (usually on the back of a check)
7. merchandise — favor shown in granting a payment delay for a specific period of time
8. to start a tab — percentage one pays on outstanding balances
9. remittance — not on time; late
10. to endorse — to be added periodically
11. to settle the account — to make known the receipt of
12. to incur — a bill of goods purchased
13. track record — to bring upon oneself
14. to accrue — days covered in a billing statement
15. overdue — payment

Can you figure out the meaning of the italicized words in the following passages?

Conversation One:

RUPERT: This is Dr. Noland's office calling to tell you that payment of your *invoice* is *overdue*. You'll *incur* late charges if you don't pay within 30 days.

MARCUS: But I paid that bill and received an *acknowledgment* of payment from your office.

RUPERT: Oops! You're right. Please forgive me.

Conversation Two:

PAUL: Would you like *to start a tab* for the *merchandise* you are buying while staying at the hotel?

MRS. REEVES: Yes, that would be helpful.

PAUL: When you're finished, let me know and we'll *settle the account*. All you'll have to do is *endorse* this bill with your signature.

MRS. REEVES: And the front desk will give me my *receipt* for purchases when I check out?

Short Talk:

I just received my credit card bill for the *billing cycle* ending January 31 and have a question. I've been billed for *finance charges* that I've *incurred* for not paying my previous bill on time, although I did pay it. Even if my *remittance* was received after the due date, there's still a seven day *grace period* that should have been applied. I have an excellent *track record* of on-time payments. There is no reason I should *accrue* finance or any other charges, and I refuse to pay them.

Fill in the blanks to complete the sentences:

16. Customers who do not pay their bills on time will _____ late charges.

17. You must _____ the back of this check with your signature before I can cash it for you.

18. Unpaid balances on credit cards will result in _____ _____, which keep adding up until you pay off your bill.

19. Business-related _____ must be submitted to accounting by the end of each month if reimbursement is requested.

20. Bob has the best _____ of anyone I know when it comes to paying bills. He pays every bill the day he gets it.

21. _____ is due 30 days after receiving this invoice.

22. I'm tired of getting this bill every month. I want to _____ by paying off my balance.

23. Interest will _____ on any outstanding balance not paid before or on the due date.

24. _____ can be paid for with cash, credit card, or money order.

25. Had it not been for the _____, my payment would have been late and I would have had to pay a late charge.

26. The clerk will _____ for us and we can pay for everything we bought altogether when we leave the shop.

27. We'll send you an _____ of your payment once we receive the check in the mail.

28. Since there are 30 days in this month and we bill monthly, your _____ will cover 30 days.

29. Payments that are not received by the due date are considered _____.

30. Send me an _____ for the subscription and I'll pay the bill when I receive it.

Answer Key

1. to make known the receipt of

2. favor shown in granting a payment delay for a specific period of time

3. days covered in a billing statement

4. a bill of goods purchased

5. proof of purchase or payment

6. percentage one pays on outstanding balances

7. goods that are bought and sold

8. to have things you will buy listed for payment all at once when you are finished buying

9. payment

10. to sign one's name (usually on the back of a check)

11. to pay what you owe

12. to bring upon oneself

13. history of behavior

14. to be added periodically

15. not on time; late

16. incur

17. endorse

18. finance charges

19. receipts

20. track record

21. remittance

22. to settle the account

23. accrue

24. merchandise

25. grace period

26. start a tab

27. acknowledgment

28. billing cycle

29. overdue

30. invoice

4 Board Meeting

Match each word or phrase to its meaning:

1. motion — to assemble for a meeting
2. minutes — a proposal
3. to adjourn — to put in order of importance
4. resolution — to postpone consideration of a proposal
5. to convene — to come up with ideas
6. bylaws — a formal statement of a decision made
7. to carry out — to approve
8. to prioritize — rules for how the board is structured and conducts itself
9. to table a motion — to start a meeting
10. quorum — to end the meeting
11. chairman — to put into practice
12. to brainstorm — a formal record of a meeting
13. to pass — to occur
14. to take place — minimum number of members required to be present before business can be conducted
15. to call to order — leader of the board

Can you figure out the meaning of the italicized words in the following passages?

Conversation One:

KEVIN: Did you see the *minutes* of the last board meeting? The *bylaws* were revised to reflect the company's new mission and vision.

OLIVIA: The board has developed an ambitious strategic plan. I agree with the new focus.

KEVIN: The problem is that the board did not have a *quorum* when the vote was held.

Conversation Two:

OLIVIA: The *chairman* of the board *convened* an emergency meeting to discuss the president's sudden resignation from the company.

KEVIN: I heard the board *brainstormed* for hours about how to handle the situation.

OLIVIA: One member even made a *motion* to dissolve the company. They *tabled that motion* indefinitely.

KEVIN: They finally *passed* a *resolution* to *prioritize* the duties *carried out* by the president and assigned the most important tasks to senior staff.

Short Talk:

As the new *chairman* of the board, I *call to order* my first meeting as leader of the board. Since our next meeting will take place on Thursday, I want you all to think about the *priorities* of the board so you can come to the meeting prepared. Then we'll go over these goals and discuss how we can best work together to accomplish them. Meeting is *adjourned.*

Fill in the blanks to complete the sentences:

16. Because the _____ is the person who runs the meetings and leads the board, it is important that he or she be elected by the members of the board.

17. When we _____, we lay out what we believe to be the most pressing matters that have to be dealt with.

18. _____ provide structure and guidelines for boards to follow.

19. Board meetings _____ on the first Wednesday of every month in the board room.

20. A _____ was made to extend term limits to three years as part of a plan to keep experienced members on the board.

21. For those of you who were unable to attend last time, I suggest you read the _____ from that meeting.

22. We will _____ that motion until our next meeting when we have more time to focus on that subject.

23. A _____ is made when board members want to make a formal statement of their position on an issue.

24. Let's _____ and come up with as many ideas as we can about how we might diversify our fundraising efforts.

25. I think we've covered all the items on our agenda. If there's nothing else left to discuss, this meeting is _____.

26. We will _____ in the board room at 3:00 to meet the new president of the company.

27. Meetings do not officially begin until the chairman announces a _____.

28. A _____ is required at the board meeting in order for the board to vote on proposals.

29. In order _____ your duties as a board member, you must attend each meeting and come prepared.

30. The vote was _____ because the majority of the members supported the proposal.

Answer Key

1. a proposal
2. a formal record of a meeting
3. to end the meeting
4. a formal statement of a decision made
5. to assemble for a meeting
6. rules for how the board is structured and conducts itself
7. to put into practice
8. to put in order of importance
9. to postpone consideration of a proposal
10. minimum number of members required to be present before business can be conducted
11. leader of the board
12. to come up with ideas
13. to approve
14. to occur
15. to start a meeting
16. chairman
17. prioritize
18. bylaws
19. take place
20. motion
21. minutes
22. table
23. resolution
24. brainstorm
25. adjourned
26. convene
27. call to order
28. quorum
29. to carry out
30. passed

5 Business Planning

Match each word or phrase to its meaning:

1. goal	anything used to accomplish a definite purpose
2. lead-time	a definite piece of work to be done
3. to extend	to bring to a successful conclusion
4. long-range	a plan or program of action
5. tool	changed
6. to propose	time to prepare; advance notice
7. task	having no purpose
8. revised	allowing for the more distant future
9. deadline	the latest time to finish something
10. to accomplish	the result toward which effort is directed
11. to achieve	to create from existing ideas
12. meaningless	able to function or be used
13. scheme	to get through effort
14. operational	to prolong or lengthen
15. to devise	to offer for consideration

Can you figure out the meaning of the italicized words in the following passages?

Conversation One:

GRETA: The *long-range goals* we set for our department need to be revised.

JONATHAN: You mean since we can't meet the short-range ones?

GRETA: Yes, that, and the fact that our competition has already *achieved* what we planned to do in five years.

Conversation Two:

JONATHAN: There's not enough *lead-time* to submit a well-thought-out *proposal*.

GRETA: I'll try to get the *deadline extended*.

JONATHAN: That would be helpful, but we also don't have the *tools* we need to *accomplish* the *task*.

GRETA: I'll get you whatever resources you need. It's important that this *proposal* be a winning one.

Small Talk:

You've known me long enough to know I won't waste your time with *meaningless tasks*. But we need to stop what we're doing and think about what we want to do. We need to *devise* some strategies to make our workplace more efficient and our business more competitive. We need to develop an *operational scheme* that will carry us into the next century and will put us on top of the competition.

Fill in the blanks to complete the sentences:

16. A successful business plan starts with laying out the _____ you wish to accomplish.

17. A _____ conversation is one that is lacking in sincerity and substance.

18. We must _____ a method for handling inquiries in a more efficient manner.

19. Since there was no way we would finish the project on time, we had to get the deadline _____.

20. He _____ a great deal of success with the company and was promoted to vice president.

21. Your _____ is to develop a timeline for the project, which we will then discuss.

22. Policies need to be reviewed and _____ every couple of years to reflect changes in the company.

23. This _____ provides a plan for how we will cut expenses and increase revenues in the next five years.

24. You can _____ anything if you put your mind to it.

25. We need to be prepared for the future and develop a _____ business plan.

26. The _____ for establishing a team-building program for employees was submitted to the board for review and approval.

27. With the right _____, I can design a high-quality, professional brochure.

28. If I have proper _____ to prepare, I'm sure I can produce a thorough presentation.

29. Is this computer _____? It's making a terrible noise.

30. The conference registration _____ has passed; the last day to register was yesterday.

Answer Key

1. the result toward which effort is directed

2. time to prepare; advanced notice

3. to prolong or lengthen

4. allowing for the more distant future

5. anything used to accomplish a definite purpose

6. to offer for consideration

7. a definite piece of work to be done

8. changed

9. the latest time to finish something

10. to bring to a successful conclusion

11. to get through effort

12. having no purpose

13. a plan or program of action

14. able to function or be used

15. to create from existing ideas

16. goals

17. meaningless

18. devise

19. extended

20. achieved

21. task

22. revised

23. scheme

24. accomplish

25. long-range

26. proposal

27. tools

28. lead-time

29. operational

30. deadline

6 Committees

Match each word or phrase to its meaning:

1. to run late — to rest

2. agenda — to be a good match; to fill the necessary criteria

3. points — to concentrate on

4. to take a break — to not be on time

5. mission — to lessen or make easier to endure

6. in light of — suggestion

7. to fit the bill — a list of things to be acted on at a meeting

8. to focus on — basis; essence of the matter

9. colleague — for this special purpose only

10. recommendation — main ideas or issues

11. to reconvene — general agreement or harmony

12. crux — to reassemble or come back together for a meeting

13. consensus — the main purpose of an organization

14. to alleviate — an associate in an office or profession

15. ad hoc — in relation to

Can you figure out the meaning of the italicized words in the following passages?

Conversation One:

BORIS: *In light of* the growing demands made on the board of directors, an *ad hoc* committee has been formed to *focus on* recruitment of new board members.

SONIA: That's right, we need to recruit members who are dedicated to our *mission*.

BORIS: Please think about who you know who might *fit the bill*, such as your *colleagues*, and make *recommendations* for potential new members at the next meeting.

Conversation Two:

SONIA: *Take a break* and we'll *reconvene* in ten minutes. When we come back, we'll try to agree on the issues.

BORIS: Getting this group to come to an agreement will be almost impossible.

SONIA: I was hoping that this informal setting would help *alleviate* the pressure of all we need to accomplish.

BORIS: I'm sure once we get to the *crux* of the disagreement, we'll be able to move forward and build a *consensus* among members.

Short Talk:

We're *running late*, so let's get down to business. The first item of business is to approve the *agenda* for the meeting. You'll see we have a number of *points* to cover in a short period of time. We need to stay *focused* and leave this meeting with specific *recommendations* for the board's review and vote. Does everyone agree on the *agenda*?

Fill in the blanks to complete the sentences:

16. We've been working for five hours straight on this project. It's time to _____ and get some fresh air.

17. _____ the recent concerns expressed by members of the board, we will hold a special meeting to discuss the issues raised.

18. The _____ for the meeting lays out the topics we will discuss tonight.

19. The main _____ we need to address are fundraising, public awareness, and community action.

20. Committees are responsible for focusing on specific areas and making _____ to the board.

21. Ms. Talbot called to say she knows the meeting was at four o'clock but she's _____, and should be here shortly.

22. Our agency is committed to our _____ of making the community a better place in which to work and live.

23. Every year, we form an _____ committee whose sole purpose is to plan the annual fundraising benefit.

24. In order to _____ the stress of long work days, it's important to take a number of small breaks throughout the day.

25. My _____ are taking me to dinner after work to celebrate our first year of working together.

26. Individuals who promise to be active members and to fulfill our needs and requirements will _____.

27. Reaching a _____ and getting people with different opinions to agree is challenging.

28. Meetings that _____ the issues at hand and don't go off on tangents are the most productive.

29. Once you identify the _____ of the matter, the root of the problem, you are better equipped to come up with solutions.

30. After lunch, we'll _____ the meeting and get back to work.

Answer Key

1. to not be on time

2. a list of things to be acted on at a meeting

3. main ideas or issues

4. to rest

5. the main purpose of an organization

6. in relation to

7. to be a good match; to fill the necessary criteria

8. to concentrate on

9. an associate in an office or profession

10. suggestion

11. to reassemble or come back together for a meeting

12. basis; essence of the matter

13. general agreement or harmony

14. to lessen or make easier to endure

15. for this special purpose only

16. take a break

17. in light of

18. agenda

19. points

20. recommendations

21. running late

22. mission

23. ad hoc

24. alleviate

25. colleagues

26. fit the bill

27. consensus

28. focus on

29. crux

30. reconvene

7 Computers

Match each word or phrase to its meaning:

1.	to scroll	search of the World Wide Web
2.	to download	computer programs
3.	software	to prepare disk for data storage
4.	configuration	a caret (>) or box that requires a user to make a choice
5.	to reboot	choice
6.	Web search	to move up or down a list
7.	to upgrade	settings needed for computer to work properly
8.	modem	part of computer where information and files are stored
9.	to format	to erase
10.	disk	to improve
11.	prompt	a thin, flat plate for saving computer files
12.	menu	device for transmitting computer data over telephone lines
13.	to delete	to save an electronic file from one computer to another
14.	hard drive	list of options
15.	option	to restart the computer

Can you figure out the meaning of the italicized words in the following passages?

Conversation One:

LEWIS: I was *downloading* a file to my *hard drive* when my computer crashed. I was so worried I'd lose all my files. And I had to start all over with my *Web search* to find the application I was trying to *download*.

PREETI: Oh no. What did you do?

LEWIS: I *rebooted* the computer and crossed my fingers.

Conversation Two:

PREETI: I ordered a new CPU, monitor, and *modem* from a really neat online service. I love electronic commerce.

LEWIS: What if the computer were damaged or needed service? Aren't you worried you couldn't return it?

PREETI: Not really. All the equipment is under warranty, and comes *configured* and loaded with *software*.

LEWIS: I need to *upgrade* the system in my home office. Could give me the address of the online service?

Short Talk:

In this computer training class, we'll begin with the basics. First, we'll *format* a *disk*. We can do so by typing the command "format a:\" at the c:\ *prompt*. Or, as an alternative method of formatting, we can go to the special *menu* and *scroll* down to "erase *disk*." Both of these methods will automatically *delete* any files already stored on the disk you are formatting. Don't worry, though; you'll be given the option to cancel or proceed with the formatting before these files get erased.

Fill in the blanks to complete the sentences:

16. With the pace of technological advances, I'd have to _____ my computer on a monthly basis to stay current.

17. When you install the new modem in your computer, you'll need to _____ the software settings for the e-mail connection.

18. The World Wide Web is so vast, it takes me forever to navigate through it. Last night, I spent two hours doing a simple _____ for information on the weather.

19. Nancy saved my report on this floppy _____, which I think is corrupt because I can't seem to open the file.

20. This new and improved _____ can dial in over standard phone lines at speeds faster than you'd ever imagine.

21. Have you seen the _____ application that allows you to translate your documents into Japanese?

22. After I accidentally deleted my document, I set my computer to _____ me to save my work every ten minutes.

23. The disk won't read; you have to _____ it for your computer.

24. The file _____ provides you with a list of options for page setup and printing.

25. I don't like to have to _____ all the time—but when the computer freezes, what else can you do but turn it off and on?

26. The _____ in my computer can store up to 2 gigabytes of data, games, and software programs.

27. The easiest way to erase text you don't want is to highlight it and press the _____ key.

28. The message box on my monitor says, "Try Again" or "Quit;" which _____ should I choose?

29. You can access the president's speech by connecting to the White House Web site and _____ the speech file.

30. Pressing on the up or down arrows will allow you to _____ through the list of documents.

Success with Business Words

Answer Key

1. to move up or down a list
2. to save an electronic file from one computer to another
3. computer programs
4. settings needed for computer to work properly
5. to restart the computer
6. search of the World Wide Web
7. to improve
8. device for transmitting computer data over telephone lines
9. to prepare disk for data storage
10. a thin, flat plate for saving computer files
11. a caret (>) or box that requires user to make a choice
12. list of options
13. to erase
14. part of computer where information and files are stored
15. choice

16. upgrade
17. configure
18. Web search
19. disk
20. modem
21. software
22. prompt
23. format
24. menu
25. reboot
26. hard drive
27. delete
28. option
29. downloading
30. scroll

8 | Conferences

Match each word or phrase to its meaning:

1. in attendance — the act of giving a speech or providing information in a formal way

2. key note — the most important points

3. representative — prepared statements distributed for informational purposes

4. presentation — celebrated, marked by excellence

5. audience — a number of related talks read or delivered in sessions before a group

6. to jot down — a person who speaks or acts on behalf of an organization

7. highlights — to write down

8. no problem — not to be published or quoted

9. delegation — to be present

10. handouts — without difficulty or inconvenience

11. workshop — a group of persons designated to act for or represent another or others

12. distinguished — small desk with a microphone and slanted top for papers to rest on

13. off the record — the listeners or viewers collectively

14. series of lectures — a seminar that emphasizes exchange of ideas and demonstration of skills

15. podium — the speaker or speech that embodies the main theme of a conference

Can you figure out the meaning of the italicized words in the following passages?

Conversation One:

HANK: The *key note* speaker gave an interesting speech. Her *presentation* was the best I think I've seen.

JUDY: Not only did she have a lively multimedia *presentation*, she engaged the *audience*.

HANK: I like the way she invited the *audience* to take part in the presentation by asking many questions.

Conversation Two:

JUDY: Each department is sending a *representative* to the international trade *workshop* next week. I'd like you to go.

HANK: I'd love to go. *Delegations* from almost every country will be *in attendance* to share their experiences.

JUDY: I'd like you to submit a report of the *highlights* of the conference, so be sure to *jot down* notes and get all the *handouts* that accompany the sessions.

Short Talk:

Welcome to the third in our *series of lectures* by *distinguished* speakers from around the country. Before our speaker for this session comes up the *podium*, I want to remind you that the speaker chooses to speak *off the record* so that he may speak candidly without fear that the press will misquote him. I'm now proud to introduce Dr. Leonardo Noto, a leader in the field of environmental conservation. Dr. Noto has a fascinating background and is here to share with us the results of his latest study of biodiversity and the rain forests.

Fill in the blanks to complete the sentences:

16. When we realized there would be many more people _____ than initially expected, we had to reserve a larger room for the event.

17. Speakers prefer to use a _____, which allows them to read from their papers without distracting the audience.

18. The _____ would have been more interesting if the speaker had prepared what he was going to say beforehand.

19. It would be _____ for me to carry that box for you.

20. If the _____ asks a lot of questions and laughs at your jokes, you know your presentation was successful.

21. Her _____ career began when she was appointed president of a multinational company at the youthful age of thirty.

22. I don't have time to read the report from the conference, so give me the _____.

23. A German trade _____ will be visiting the United States to promote the government's new trade policies and incentives.

24. Having _____ of the presentations makes it easier to pay attention, because you don't have to worry about taking notes.

25. I learned so much at the writer's _____, where there was sharing of ideas and skill-building sessions.

26. Let me _____ your address so I can send you the conference report when it's released.

27. A _____ will be available to answer any questions about the agency and its policies.

28. I don't want to be quoted on this, so _____, I think the speech was poorly written and poorly delivered.

29. A _____ speaker should be someone who's well known and can address the major themes of the conference.

30. A _____ on doing business over the Internet will be held throughout the month.

Success with Business Words

Answer Key

1. to be present
2. the speaker or speech that embodies the main theme of a conference
3. a person who speaks or acts on behalf of an organization
4. the act of giving a speech or providing information in a formal way
5. the listeners or viewers collectively
6. to write down
7. the most important points
8. without difficulty or inconvenience
9. a group of persons designated to act for or represent another or others
10. prepared statements distributed for informational purposes
11. a seminar that emphasizes exchange of ideas and the demonstration of skills
12. celebrated, marked by excellence
13. not to be published or quoted
14. a number of related talks read or delivered in sessions before a group
15. small desk with a microphone and slanted top for papers to rest on
16. in attendance
17. podium
18. presentation
19. no problem
20. audience
21. distinguished
22. highlights
23. delegation
24. handouts
25. workshop
26. jot down
27. representative
28. off the record
29. key note
30. series of lectures

KAPLAN

9 Contracts

Match each word or phrase to its meaning:

1. contract	to agree
2. parties	to indicate or suggest without express statement
3. null and void	pointed out
4. clause	having obligation
5. annulled	holder or owner of shares; person who has a stake in something
6. to enter into an agreement	without legal force
7. to authorize	benefit; gain
8. shareholder	groups gathered for a specific purpose
9. to imply	to give power to act, judge, or command
10. indicated	part of an article or document, as a distinct provision of law
11. reasonable	an agreement enforceable by law
12. terms	cancelled
13. to expire	logical; fair
14. binding	conditions and stipulations
15. advantage	to terminate or run out

Can you figure out the meaning of the italicized words in the following passages?

Conversation One:

URSULA: According to this *contract*, if we do not meet any of the *terms*, the contract is *null and void*.

ELEANOR: Yes, but we can insert a *clause* giving you a ten-day grace period. When the grace period *expires*, the contract is *annulled*.

URSULA: We should also add a clause regarding arbitration of differences.

Conversation Two:

URSULA: I don't want to *imply* that every point in this contract is negotiable.

ELEANOR: Of course not. A *contract* exists to protect both parties. Some sections of the contract cannot be negotiated.

URSULA: I'm glad to see you're being *reasonable*.

ELEANOR: However, I have *indicated* those parts of the *contract* that are not to the *advantage* of my client.

Small Talk:

Only the CEO, the president, and the members of the Executive Committee of the Board of Directors are *authorized* to *enter into an agreement* and sign legally *binding* contracts. The *terms* of the contract must be reviewed by the legal department and approved by the *shareholders* before the contract can be signed by the officers.

Fill in the blanks to complete the sentences:

16. The contract _____ one year after it was first signed.

17. I didn't mean to _____ you were not representing my best interests.

18. While I'm away from the office, you will be _____ to make decisions on my behalf.

19. In order to make sure we're both legally protected, we'll draw up a _____.

20. I'd like to add a _____ to the contract that I'm not responsible for damage to the property caused by acts of nature.

21. The employment contract was _____ because the employer failed to meet the terms of the agreement.

22. We found the terms _____ and fair, so we accepted the offer.

23. If you _____ a contract, you are required to live up to your end of it.

24. If you agree to all the _____ laid out in the contract, sign here.

25. All staff, volunteers, and others who have purchased stock are _____ and have a say in major decisions.

26. Both of the _____ came to the table ready to make a deal.

27. It's to your _____ to read over all the materials before signing them.

28. Earlier, you _____ that you wanted to consult an attorney; are you still interested in doing that?

29. One of the parties refused to sign the contract, making it _____.

30. A _____ contract obligates you to fulfill the terms and is a promise that cannot be broken.

Answer Key

1. an agreement enforceable by law

2. groups gathered for a specific purpose

3. without legal force

4. part of an article or document, as a distinct provision of law

5. cancelled

6. to agree

7. to give power to act, judge, or command

8. holder or owner of shares; person who has a stake in something

9. to indicate or suggest without express statement

10. pointed out

11. logical; fair

12. conditions and stipulations

13. to terminate or run out

14. having obligation

15. benefit; gain

16. expired

17. imply

18. authorized

19. contract

20. clause

21. annulled

22. reasonable

23. enter into

24. terms

25. shareholders

26. parties

27. advantage

28. indicated

29. null and void

30. binding

10 E-Mail

Match each word or phrase to its meaning:

1. online
   separate document sent with e-mail message

2. attachment
   more than one recipient

3. Internet service provider
   not easily accessed

4. to redirect
   the act of examining something to determine the problem

5. to diagnose
   to decrease

6. to get through to
   to make personal

7. undeliverable
   to add text to existing document

8. to take away
   to send to a different recipient

9. multiple addresses
   to return to sender

10. to personalize
    connected to other computers by modem

11. connection
    to send message from one computer to another

12. to insert
    two computers communicating with each other

13. to bounce back
    to establish a connection

14. to forward
    company that sells Internet service

15. inaccessible
    not able to be delivered

Can you figure out the meaning of the italicized words in the following passages?

Conversation One:

ALAN: E-mail is a great invention. I can e-mail letters to all my family and friends around the world at one time using *multiple addresses*.

DIANE: I don't use e-mail for letters to friends and family, because it *takes away* the personal touch that hand-written letters and phone calls have.

ALAN: I guess you're right; you can *personalize* the address of the recipient, but that's about all.

Conversation Two:

DIANE: My e-mail bounced back as *undeliverable*.

ALAN: Usually that means that something is wrong with the address.

DIANE: I hope you can *diagnose* the problem. All I did was *insert* and *remove* some text from an e-mail I wrote and *redirected* it, with an *attachment*, to this address.

ALAN: You forgot to finish typing in the address to which you want the e-mail *redirected*. Try *forwarding* your returned e-mail to the full address.

Short Talk:

I need to find an *Internet service provider* that allows me to go *online* and make a *connection* right away. My current provider is *inaccessible* during the day because it has so many users. I can never get through during business hours. I never thought I'd rely so heavily on e-mail, but it's fast and inexpensive compared to long-distance and international calling.

Fill in the blanks to complete the sentences:

16. Nancy was relieved when the angry message she had sent to her boss _____ to her.

17. My friends _____ me all kinds of e-mail jokes they receive from their co-workers.

18. If a message is too long to put in an e-mail message, you can send it as an _____.

19. E-mail allows you to _____ many people quickly, easily, and inexpensively.

20. You can _____ your own comments in an e-mail someone has sent you by typing them into the existing text.

21. A good _____ will set up your e-mail account and provide uninterrupted online service.

22. Let me take a look at your computer, and I should be able to _____ the problem.

23. When my e-mail was returned to me as _____, I realized I had mistyped the address.

24. I set up an address list of online newsletter subscribers so I can send the newsletter to _____ and reach everyone at once.

25. The significant increase in the use of e-mail _____ revenue from post office and long distance telephone service providers.

26. I'm sorry my telephone was busy. I was _____ checking and sending e-mails.

27. I _____ my messages by ending each e-mail with my favorite quote.

28. While our computer system is down, you will not be able to use online services and e-mail will be _____.

29. When you make a _____ to the service provider, a box will appear on your screen that says "successful login."

30. If you get an e-mail that is not meant for you, please _____ it to the proper recipient.

Answer Key

1. connected to other computers by modem

2. separate document sent with e-mail message

3. company that sells Internet service

4. to send to a different recipient

5. the act of examining something to determine the problem

6. to establish a connection

7. not able to be delivered

8. to decrease

9. more than one recipient

10. to make personal

11. two computers communicating with each other

12. to add text to existing document

13. to return to sender

14. to send message from one computer to another

15. not easily accessed

16. bounced back

17. forward

18. attachment

19. get through to

20. insert

21. Internet service provider

22. diagnose

23. undeliverable

24. multiple addresses

25. takes away

26. online

27. personalize

28. inaccessible

29. connection

30. redirect

11 Faxes

Match each word or phrase to its meaning:

1. automatically   to transmit widely

2. header   person who receives

3. error report   two machines making a connection

4. confirmation report   list of incoming and outgoing faxes

5. short cut   report that is printed when your fax transmitted successfully

6. to broadcast   text that appears at top of each page

7. transmission log   report printed when the fax doesn't transmit; error in transmission

8. format   self-acting

9. recipient   the first page of a fax containing identifying information

10. face down   the general appearance of a publication or document

11. transmission   text side of paper that faces down (blank side faces up)

12. handshake   to make known

13. cover sheet   as soon as possible

14. ASAP   a shorter or quicker method than the usual method

15. to identify   the process of sending from one person, place, or thing to another

Can you figure out the meaning of the italicized words in the following passages?

Conversation One:

SARAH: Would you please fax me a copy of the proposal so I can review it before our meeting tomorrow?

LARRY: I'll send it *ASAP*. I'll use a *cover sheet* to *identify* you as the *recipient*.

Conversation Two:

SARAH: This fax machine has been giving me trouble all day. I can't get the fax to go through and keep getting these *error reports* telling me the *transmission* failed.

LARRY: Remember, place the document *face down*.

SARAH: It is face down. The fax machine dials, I press the start transmission button, and then nothing happens.

LARRY: I see the problem. You have to wait for the *handshake*, and then press the start button.

Short Talk:

Faxing is still the best way to send and receive documents quickly when you want to ensure the documents are received in their original *format*. Fax machines now also have a variety of options that allows users more flexibility. You can program your company's name and fax number to be the *header*, which will appear at the top of each fax you send, making it easy for *recipients* to *identify* the sender. *Short cut* features such as *broadcast* faxing allow users to send the same fax to a pre-programmed list of *recipients*. Most fax machines print *confirmation reports* and *transmission logs automatically* to help users track the status of fax *transmissions*.

Fill in the blanks to complete the sentences:

16. When sending the same fax to many people, it's best to use the _____ feature.

17. The office manager programmed the fax machine to _____ send the document after hours to get cheaper long-distance rates.

18. This fax _____ consists of ten pages, which you should be receiving any minute now.

19. The person to whom you are sending the fax is the _____.

20. When a fax transmission fails, the machine prints an _____ _____ to let you know the fax did not go through.

21. The first page of the fax, or the _____, typically includes the name of the sender and recipient, the date, and number of pages in the fax transmission.

22. So that we may easily _____ the recipient, please include his or her name on the cover sheet of the fax.

23. You'l know when you get a _____ because you'll hear the sound of your machine connecting with the other machine.

24. Place the side of the paper with the text _____ in the fax machine when sending a document.

25. The _____ is a list of all incoming and outgoing faxes; it allows us to keep track of the flow of faxes.

26. We programmed our fax machine to print a _____ on every page that includes our company's name and fax number.

27. I know a _____ that will save you time so you can finish this project quickly and go home.

28. We need to meet the 2:30 deadline. I need the information you promised _____ so I can include it in the report.

29. The _____ of this report is difficult to read. Changing the font and the spacing of the text should help.

30. The _____ will verify the document has been transmitted successfully.

Answer Key

1. self-acting
2. text that appears at top of each page
3. report that is printed when the fax doesn't transmit; error in transmission
4. report that is printed when your fax transmitted successfully
5. a shorter or quicker method than the usual method
6. to transmit widely
7. list of incoming and outgoing faxes
8. the general appearance of a publication or document
9. person who receives
10. text side of paper that faces down (blank side faces up)
11. the process of sending from one person, place, or thing to another
12. two machines making a connection
13. the first page of a fax containing identifying information
14. as soon as possible
15. to make known
16. broadcast
17. automatically
18. transmission
19. recipient
20. error report
21. cover sheet
22. identify
23. handshake
24. face down
25. transmission log
26. header
27. short cut
28. ASAP
29. format
30. confirmation report

12 Finance

Match each word or phrase to its meaning:

1.	profit	to take for granted; to suppose
2.	either way	comparative relation between two things in size, amount, etcetera
3.	equity	ending involvement; leaving
4.	to assume	anything brought about by a cause; result
5.	expense	compulsory payment of a percentage of income, property, etcetera
6.	effect	a financial cost
7.	proportion	anything producing an effect or result
8.	revenue	expressed in a definite way
9.	actual	regardless of the option chosen, the result is the same
10.	cause	income
11.	tax	money or property owned or used in business
12.	capital	the sum remaining after deducting costs
13.	formulated	property owned
14.	holdings	existing in reality
15.	to get out	the value of property beyond the amount owed on it

Can you figure out the meaning of the italicized words in the following passages?

Conversation One:

GAVIN: Our company has a great deal of *equity* in its buildings and real estate *holdings*, but has little working *capital*.

ANITA: Its *revenues* are enormous, so I *assume* the *actual profits* are small.

GAVIN: Yes. Unfortunately, the *expenses* are almost as enormous as the revenues.

Conversation Two:

GAVIN: Rising interest rates are a result of rising inflation.

ANITA: I thought it was the other way around.

GAVIN: It's hard to determine which is the *cause* and which is the *effect*.

ANITA: *Either way*, I'm *getting out* of the stock market and putting my money in bonds.

Small Talk:

A corporation is taxed on its corporate income, which is *revenue* minus *expenses*. Accountants have *formulated* ways to make revenue look smaller and expenses look greater, thus reducing the amount of *taxes* a corporation may have to pay. For example, there are deductible expenses such as business equipment, buildings, and employee-related expenses like salaries and benefits. These expenses can be *proportionally* deducted from a corporation's *revenues*, which will decrease the total *profit* and the total *tax* to be paid.

Fill in the blanks to complete the sentences:

16. You can spend the interest on the money you've invested, but never touch the _____.

17. Telephone service, payroll, and rent are just some of our monthly _____.

18. I could take a loan from the bank or borrow the money from a friend; _____, I'll have to pay interest.

19. Our _____ would be much higher if our expenses were lower.

20. When you make an _____, you're making a judgment based on what you believe to be true and not necessarily one based on facts.

21. The company has _____ a strategy to make better use of its resources.

22. We need to find out the _____ of the budget deficit before we can get rid of it.

23. We sold our stock _____ when we heard the market was in trouble.

24. There's too much risk involved in trading; I'm _____ of the profession.

25. The longer you pay mortgage on your home, the more _____ you build up.

26. Add up the receipts for the expenses for the year and give me the _____ amount we spent.

27. The government imposed a _____ on all sales in order to increase its revenue.

28. Growth in the economy has a positive _____ on employment rates.

29. Our records show that our client base and revenues have increased _____.

30. The majority of the government's _____ comes from taxes.

Answer Key

1. the sum remaining after deducting costs

2. regardless of the option chosen, the result is the same

3. the value of property beyond the amount owed on it

4. to take for granted; to suppose

5. a financial cost

6. anything brought about by a cause; result

7. comparative relation between two things in size, amount, etcetera

8. income

9. existing in reality

10. anything producing an effect or result

11. compulsory payment of a percentage of income, property, value, etcetera

12. money or property owned or used in business

13. expressed in a definite way

14. property owned

15. to end involvement; to leave

16. capital

17. expenses

18. either way

19. profits

20. assumption

21. formulated

22. cause

23. holdings

24. getting out

25. equity

26. actual

27. tax

28. effect

29. proportionally

30. revenue

13 Hiring Personnel

Match each word or phrase to its meaning:

1. applicants	people who know and will testify to one's character and abilities
2. appointment	the steps taken when identifying candidates for employment
3. résumé	to be able to talk about
4. to speak to	skills or qualities that fit a person for a job or position
5. interview	to include as one of the important factors in making a decision
6. references	to be ready to take action
7. qualifications	to examine in order to select or reject
8. to make an offer	an agreement to meet at a certain date and time
9. selection process	to limit in number
10. to take into consideration	persons who apply for a position
11. to screen	the feelings you get when you first meet a person
12. to be in a position	to put to practical use
13. first impression	a formal meeting in which a person questions or evaluates another
14. to utilize	to give a candidate a job
15. to narrow down	a summary of one's background submitted in application for a job

Can you figure out the meaning of the italicized words in the following passages?

Conversation One:

SUSAN: I'm calling because I received your impressive résumé and would like to set up an interview with you.

IRENE: I have a number of *appointments* on Monday, but am available on Tuesday at 11 A.M.

SUSAN: That's fine. Please bring with you a list of your *references*, people who can *speak to* your work record.

Conversation Two:

SUSAN: We've received many *résumés* in response to our ad.

ED: How will you *screen* all those who applied? Will you *be in a position to* fill the opening in time?

SUSAN: I've already screened the *applicants* and have *narrowed down* the list to the ten with the best *qualifications*. I'll *interview* them next week.

ED: The *selection process* is sure to be a difficult one, since the top ten all seem to be excellent candidates.

Short Talk:

Thank you for meeting with me last week to discuss the position of research associate. I enjoyed learning more about the position and your company, and appreciate the offer extended to me to join the firm. My *first impression* of the firm was very positive. Unfortunately, an overseas company has *made me an offer* that I can't refuse. I'll get to travel and have a great deal of responsibility. I've taken both offers *into consideration*, and feel my skills could be better *utilized* in an overseas environment; therefore, I must respectfully decline your offer.

Fill in the blanks to complete the sentences:

16. The personnel department will be calling your _____ to ask them about your ability and performance.

17. We're seeking _____ who are interested in the positions that are available at this time.

18. I've been offered three different positions and don't know how I'm going to _____ my choices and pick one.

19. Ms. Barber's schedule is completely booked; she has _____ with clients every day next week.

20. The _____ you get when you meet someone influences how you feel about that person.

21. I think you're the perfect candidate for the job, and I'm prepared _____.

22. If you're interested in applying for the position, send a _____, highlighting your work experience and education, to the human resources department.

23. Employers ask many questions in an _____ so they can get to know you better.

24. His _____ were exactly what we needed for the position.

25. When making a big decision, it's important _____ _____ all factors that influence your thinking.

26. Since there are hundreds of applicants and few positions, the _____ is extremely competitive.

27. The President's staff _____ all calls coming in to his office.

28. With the money I'll be making at this new job, I'll _____ buy that brand new car I've had my eye on.

29. I've never worked directly with Sally, and I'm afraid I cannot _____ her strengths and weaknesses.

30. It's a shame that someone who is so creative works in an office where his talents and skills are not fully _____.

Answer Key

1. persons who apply for a position
2. an agreement to meet at a certain date and time
3. a summary of one's background submitted in application for a job
4. to be able to talk about
5. a formal meeting in which a person questions or evaluates another
6. people who know and will testify to one's character and abilities
7. skills or qualities that fit a person for a job or position
8. to give a candidate a job
9. the steps taken when identifying candidates for employment
10. to include as one of the important factors in making a decision
11. to examine in order to select or reject
12. to be ready to take action
13. the feelings you get when you first meet a person
14. to put to practical use
15. to limit in number
16. references

17. applicants
18. narrow down
19. appointments
20. first impression
21. to make an offer
22. résumé
23. interview
24. qualifications
25. to take into consideration
26. selection process
27. screens
28. be in a position to
29. speak to
30. utilized

14 Investment

Match each word or phrase to its meaning:

1. stock — exposure to chance of injury or loss

2. shares — substantial rise in general price level

3. stockbroker — securities owned as investment

4. bond — to invest in the stocks and bonds of different companies in different industries

5. to diversify — a document describing a project or enterprise distributed to prospective innovators

6. portfolio — person with access to privileged information

7. mutual fund — a yield or profit from an investment

8. brokerage — a promise to pay; a certificate of debt to be paid by a government or corporation to an individual

9. insider — the business of a stockbroker

10. risk — outstanding capital of a corporation

11. to forecast — financially secure

12. prospectus — person who buys and sells securities

13. inflation — to state future occurrences in

14. sound — a company that invests pooled funds into a diversified list of securities

15. return — equal parts of a corporations capital stock

Can you figure out the meaning of the italicized words in the following passages?

Conversation One:

DAVE: My *stockbroker* recommends that I *diversify* my investment *portfolio* because I have all my money in one stock.

MARJORIE: That makes sense—if one decreases in value, another is likely to increase, and you'll break even.

DAVE: But which stocks are profitable? Don't you have a relative who works in *brokerage* firm who could give me some *insider* advice?

Conversation Two:

MARJORIE: Joe bought 1,000 *shares* of the company's *stock*.

DAVE: He told me he studied the company's *prospectus* in great detail, and was impressed.

MARJORIE: Market analysts *forecast* the value of the stock to triple in three months. If inflation remains low and the economy *sound*, Joe stands to make a huge *return* on his investment.

Short Talk:

If you invest your money wisely, you could retire early and live off your investment *returns*. Before you do this, you should think about how much *risk* you're willing to take. If the market takes a hit, you could risk losing your money. *Mutual funds* and securities are the most common way to invest. Mutual funds are managed by a group of fund managers who add all the investors' money together to invest in a variety of things. Securities, meanwhile, are *stocks* and *bonds*.

Fill in the blanks to complete the sentences:

16. _____ are easier to manage because a group of people do the trading for you and your money is spread among a variety of different investments, like stocks and bonds.

17. High _____ makes everything more expensive so people can't afford to buy as much as they normally would.

18. The greater the _____ you take, the greater the potential is to make a lot of money or lose it all.

19. Government _____ were issued during World War II to raise money for the war effort.

20. If the market is strong, expect a good _____ on your investment.

21. I've done research and sought financial advice, and now have the information I need to make a _____ decision.

22. He was accused of _____ trading when his boss heard him sharing confidential information with a client over the phone.

23. Financial advisors _____ continued growth in the economy and a significant decrease in unemployment over the next year.

24. _____ your holdings by investing in a variety of stocks in a number of industries.

25. My _____ sold my stocks just before the price of my shares fell to half their original value.

26. You can expand your _____ by investing in a wide range of stocks and bonds.

27. After reviewing the corporation's _____, we decided not to invest because its performance history was not so good.

28. Stockbrokers specialize in _____, the buying and selling stocks and bonds on behalf of their clients.

29. In an attempt to raise money for major capital improvements, the corporation issued _____ to public investors.

30. The price of the software company's _____ soared to $100 a share with the release of their newest video game.

Answer Key

1. the outstanding capital of a corporation

2. equal parts of a corporation's capital stock

3. person who buys and sells securities

4. a promise to pay; a certificate of debt to be paid by a government or corporation

5. to invest in the stocks and bonds of different companies in different industries

6. the securities owned for investment purposes

7. a company that invests pooled funds into a diversified list of securities

8. the business of a stockbroker

9. person who has access to privileged information

10. exposure to chance of injury or loss

11. to state expected future occurrences in

12. a document describing a project or enterprise

13. substantial rise in general price level

14. financially secure

15. a yield or profit from an investment

16. mutual funds

17. inflation

18. risk

19. bonds

20. return

21. sound

22. insider

23. forecast

24. diversify

25. stockbroker

26. portfolio

27. prospectus

28. brokerage

29. shares

30. stock

15 Labor Relations

Match each word or phrase to its meaning:

1. arbitrator   a state of strained relations

2. to boycott   the shutdown of a plant to bring workers to terms

3. impact   a shared understanding

4. picket line   a deadlock

5. stalemate   a person selected to judge a dispute

6. union   a settlement in which each side makes concessions

7. lockout   a state of distress; urgent demands

8. compromise   a line of people stationed outside a place of work to demonstrate protest

9. to strike   to meet for a common purpose

10. pressure   an association of workers to promote and protect the welfare and rights of its members

11. tension   discussions made to try to reach an agreement

12. to rally   influence or effect

13. common ground   to express strong disapproval

14. negotiations   to refuse to work until certain demands are met

15. to protest   to join together in refusing to buy or deal with so as to punish or coerce

Can you figure out the meaning of the italicized words in the following passages?

Conversation One:

CONNIE: We're at a *stalemate*. The managers won't budge and the workers are not willing to *compromise*.

BERNARD: What a bad situation. The workers want what they think is fair and the employers don't have the financial resources to meet their requests.

CONNIE: Hopefully, the independent *arbitrator* will make a judgment that both sides will respect.

Conversation Two:

CONNIE: I'm glad we finally have reached *common ground*, and the *negotiations* have concluded successfully.

BERNARD: It could've been a lot worse. Five years ago, employers staged a *lockout* when they felt *pressure* from staff to raise their hourly rates by 10 percent. They thought that would teach a lesson to employees who called in sick to *protest* the low wages.

Short Talk:

Today, the *striking* workers *rallied* in front of the building again, urging the community to *boycott* products made in the factory until a settlement is made. *Tensions* are still high and the labor *unions* are engaged in intense *negotiations* to try to come to a mutually beneficial agreement. A number of workers, who can't afford another day out of work, have crossed the *picket line* to go back to work, which may affect the *impact* of the strike.

Fill in the blanks to complete the sentences:

16. _____ can be successful if both sides are willing to listen to each other and work towards a resolution.

17. An _____ will be brought in to listen to both sides and pass a judgment on this dispute.

18. The strikers formed a _____ that prevented other employees from passing into the building.

19. Local consumers refused to buy products made by the factory in support of the _____.

20. As a member of the local _____, I know my rights will be protected.

21. Family and friends _____ with the workers in support of their demands.

22. Unions have a greater _____ than individual workers because they are negotiating on behalf of all union members.

23. When both sides refuse to compromise, a _____ results.

24. The factory staged a _____, refusing to let employees enter the building, in an effort to show them that their inappropriate actions would not be tolerated.

25. A _____ was reached when managers offered a five percent raise in response to workers' demands for a ten percent increase.

26. The workers refused to go back to work and the _____ went on for many days.

27. Strikers believed they were putting _____ on their employers and that their demands would soon be met.

28. _____ grew between the two groups when communications broke down.

29. Workers and employers found _____ when they realized they agreed on the issue of workers' compensation limits.

30. They carried signs and chanted to _____ the poor working conditions.

Answer Key

1. a person selected to judge a dispute

2. to join together in refusing to buy or deal with, so as to punish or coerce

3. influence or effect

4. a line of people stationed outside a workplace to demonstrate protest

5. a deadlock

6. an association of workers to promote and protect the rights of its members

7. the shutdown of a plant to bring workers to terms

8. a settlement in which each side makes concessions

9. to refuse to work until certain demands are met

10. a state of distress; urgent demands

11. a state of strained relations

12. to meet for a common purpose

13. a shared understanding

14. discussions made to try to reach an agreement

15. to express strong disapproval

16. negotiations

17. arbitrator

18. picket line

19. boycott

20. union

21. rally

22. impact

23. stalemate

24. lockout

25. compromise

26. strike

27. pressure

28. tensions

29. common ground

30. protest

16 Letters

Match each word or phrase to its meaning:

1. to pull together   to reply
2. to respond   folded paper container for letter
3. to proofread   main part of a letter
4. to address   manner of expression
5. to the attention of   communication by letter
6. signature   to deliver
7. stationery   to read over
8. envelope   greeting
9. salutation   to collect
10. body   writing paper and envelopes
11. to drop off   person's name written by himself or herself
12. inquiry   to write in a destination
13. style   very important
14. high priority   person to receive the letter
15. correspondence   request for information

Can you figure out the meaning of the italicized words in the following passages?

Conversation One:

RHONDA: Allen, would you please *pull together* the information for me to respond to this *inquiry* letter? This is *high priority*. I just found the inquiry on my desk and noticed it's dated three months ago.

JEFF: Wow. You should clean up your desk more often. How should the letter be *addressed*?

RHONDA: *To the attention of* Mr. Martins.

Conversation Two:

JEFF: Here's the letter for your *signature*.

RHONDA: Great, but it should be printed on our corporate *stationery*.

JEFF: Oh. Someone form the mailroom came to *drop off* an *envelope* and distracted me.

RHONDA: That's okay. I want to change the *salutation* to "Dear Mr. Martins" and the closing to "Yours sincerely" anyway.

Short Talk:

When receiving an *inquiry* for materials, it is urgent that you respond within 48 hours. Customers come first, and we need to service their requests in a professional and prompt manner. Use a friendly *style* in the *body* of your letters and *proofread* your work. Keep a photocopy of all *correspondence* to keep as a backup. If you have any questions, please contact the office manager.

Fill in the blanks to complete the sentences:

16. When Mary realized she had overlooked incoming _____, she decided to clean off her desk.

17. A formal writing _____ is used for most business correspondence.

18. This letter has lots of typos. Did you _____ your work before sending it out?

19. I need a photocopy of this _____ for the accounting department's billing records.

20. Allen addressed the _____ by hand.

21. We're running low on letterhead, so one of us needs to order _____ from the printer.

22. The letter was returned to me because it was _____ incorrectly.

23. If customers make urgent requests, we must make those requests _____ items and respond immediately.

24. Please have this package delivered by courier, and put _____ Mr. Martins on the envelope.

25. The boss' _____ is required on all correspondence generated from this office.

26. The _____ "To whom it may concern" is an example of a traditional style.

27. Would you _____ this package at the post office on your way home?

28. It is important to _____ to every inquiry within 48 hours so customers get the information they need quickly.

29. If you _____ the statistics and supporting materials, I'll draft the report.

30. There are three main parts to a letter: the salutation, the _____, and the closing.

Answer Key

1. to collect
2. to reply
3. to read over
4. to write in a destination
5. person to receive the letter
6. person's name written by himself or herself
7. writing paper and envelopes
8. folded paper container for letter
9. greeting
10. main part of a letter
11. to deliver
12. request for information
13. manner of expression
14. very important
15. communication by letter

16. correspondence
17. style
18. proofread
19. inquiry
20. envelope
21. stationery
22. addressed
23. high priority
24. to the attention of
25. signature
26. salutation
27. drop off
28. respond
29. pull together
30. body

17 Marketing

Match each word or phrase to its meaning:

1. campaign — reacting readily to influence or appeals

2. efforts — to attract or interest

3. to position — a paid public notice; an advertisement

4. to promote — to place or arrange

5. responsive — sections; parts of

6. commercial — a plan

7. target — attempts; energies

8. to appeal — to direct at

9. segments — to focus

10. analysis — essential; very important

11. strategy — a series of planned actions

12. to aim at — the process of studying the nature of something or of determining its features

13. universally — in every instance; everywhere

14. vital — an objective or goal

15. to concentrate — to further growth, presence, sales

Can you figure out the meaning of the italicized words in the following passages?

Conversation One:

NATHAN: Marketing is more than just selling or *promoting* a product.

MAUDE: It's really understanding the consumer, isn't it?

NATHAN: Right. You have to make sure consumers get what they want even before they know they need it. A good market *strategy* is *vital* to a product's success.

Conversation Two:

NATHAN: I don't think we've properly *positioned* this product.

MAUDE: I agree. We're *aiming* for too wide an audience. Our *target* is much narrower.

NATHAN: Let's look at the various population *segments* and see which were the most *responsive* to our *campaign*.

MAUDE: You'll probably find that the product *appeals* to young married couples more than it does to teenagers.

Small Talk:

If you are trying to sell apples, your marketing *efforts* will apply *universally*. But if you are trying to sell wheelchairs, you must *concentrate* your marketing *efforts* on those who would be interested in using your wheelchairs. When you watch a popular program on the television and you see *commercials* for denture wearers, you can assume that the marketing department has done an *analysis* of the viewers and that a large number of the people watching the show have false teeth.

Fill in the blanks to complete the sentences:

16. Certain _____ of the population watch more television than others.

17. A _____ will be launched to promote the new and improved product.

18. We're _____ the campaign ____ teens who buy the most snack foods.

19. We need to develop a _____ to market our services.

20. _____ are designed to deliver a message in a very short time period.

21. After careful _____ of color trends, the cosmetic company decided blue was not a popular shade for lipstick.

22. Let's focus our _____ on identifying the potential markets for this product.

23. If you want to ensure a good turnout at the event, you must _____ it every chance you get.

24. A coordinated team effort is _____ to our project's success.

25. People are more _____ to advertisements that they can identify with.

26. Credit cards have become so popular that they are _____ accepted.

27. Studies show that humorous commercials _____ more to younger audiences than older ones.

28. Telemarketing companies _____ individuals who have purchased similar products to what they're trying to sell.

29. With our expanded capacity, we are well-_____ to become the leader in our field.

30. We need to _____ and stay focused if we want to finish this report on time.

Answer Key

1. a series of planned actions
2. attempts
3. to place or arrange
4. to further growth, presence, sales, etcetera
5. reacting readily to influence or appeals
6. a paid public notice; an advertisement
7. an objective or goal
8. to attract or interest
9. sections; parts of
10. the process of studying the nature of something or of determining its features
11. a plan
12. directing at
13. in every instance; everywhere
14. essential; very important
15. to focus
16. segments
17. campaign
18. aiming (the campaign) at
19. strategy
20. commercials
21. analysis
22. efforts
23. promote
24. vital
25. responsive
26. universally
27. appeal
28. target
29. positioned
30. concentrate

18 Memos

Match each word or phrase to its meaning:

1. to distribute   to reduce

2. to introduce   process

3. policy   to refer to

4. to outline   to hand out

5. to cut back on   to give basic information

6. request   following a set and proper procedure

7. to mention   within the office

8. to submit   rigid with rules

9. procedure   succinct; expressing much in few words

10. concise   to present for consideration

11. formal   steps to follow

12. to help out   to present a new person or element

13. interoffice   to assist

14. strict   plan

15. guidelines   something asked for

Can you figure out the meaning of the italicized words in the following passages?

Conversation One:

MS. FOSTER: Would you please *distribute* this *interoffice* memo, which *introduces* a new office *policy?*

MR. MALONE: Sure, glad to *help out.*

MS. FOSTER: Thanks. The finance department is trying to *cut back on* expenses. This memo explains new *guidelines* for reducing office expenses.

Conversation Two:

MR. MALONE: Look at this memo from the personnel department *outlining* procedures for vacation policy.

MS. WILLIAMS: Oh, no. Talk about *strict guidelines.* And I just put in a *request* for two weeks.

MR. MALONE: Guess you'll be the first example of an employee using an incorrect *procedure.*

MS. WILLIAMS: Well, no one *mentioned* the new policy when I submitted the request for time off.

Short Talk:

Ms. Williams, I received your *formal request* for vacation and noticed that you didn't get proper approval. As you know, we have *introduced* a new system in order to improve productivity and be fair to all employees. The *procedures* are clearly and *concisely outlined* in yesterday's memo. Did you read it? Should I *explain* the new *procedure* to you? Please *submit* your *request* again, and get the proper signatures this time. Thank you.

Fill in the blanks to complete the sentences:

16. Every time I turn around, there's a new _____ in place.

17. Memos are less _____ than other business correspondence like letters.

18. If you provide me with the _____ for the proposal, I'll be happy to draft it for you.

19. You _____ earlier in our conversation that you're going to Europe for vacation.

20. _____ for vacation should be made two weeks in advance.

21. The _____ e-mail system is down again. No one can send messages to their colleagues.

22. I need to copy this memo and this photocopier is slow. Could you _____ and take this to the copy shop?

23. The steps you have to follow to apply for positions within the company are _____ in the employee handbook.

24. The president's new _____ will create hundreds of jobs for American workers.

25. I'm so nervous. I think I need to _____ my coffee intake.

26. _____ time sheets to the accounting office no later than the last day of the month if you want to be paid on time.

27. Would you please explain why we must have such _____ policies? I don't understand why they are so rigid.

28. The information was presented _____ in the executive summary that accompanied the report.

29. Mr. Miller will personally _____ the paychecks to each employee on payday.

30. The office manager will _____ the new receptionist to all staff members so everyone can get to know him.

Answer Key

1. to hand out
2. to present a new person or element
3. plan
4. to give basic information
5. to reduce
6. something asked for
7. to refer to
8. to present for consideration
9. process
10. succinct; expressing much in few words
11. following a set and proper procedure
12. assist
13. within the office
14. rigid with rules
15. steps to follow
16. procedure
17. formal
18. guidelines
19. mentioned
20. requests
21. interoffice
22. help me out
23. outlined
24. policy
25. cut back on
26. submit
27. strict
28. concisely
29. distribute
30. introduce

19 Mergers

Match each word or phrase to its meaning:

1.	rumor	to take in; incorporate
2.	mutual	to group resources, etcetera for some common purpose
3.	merger	sticking together
4.	infrastructure	what should be correct according to some rule or principle
5.	to absorb	gain
6.	cohesive	an unconfirmed report
7.	redundant	wealth, assets
8.	resources	to make or become whole or complete
9.	to pool	a grouping of several companies into one
10.	to integrate	taking place little by little
11.	to combine	an idea; a general notion
12.	in theory	unnecessary or excessive
13.	acquisition	to join into one
14.	gradual	done or felt by each of the parties involved
15.	concept	basic installations and facilities

Can you figure out the meaning of the italicized words in the following passages?

Conversation One:

STEVE: There's a *rumor* that our firm is going to *merge* with another law firm.

VALERIE: If that happens, we'll be the largest telecommunications law firm in the country.

STEVE: It will take a long time to *integrate* the two firms into a *cohesive* group.

Conversation Two:

STEVE: As part of the merger, we're going to *combine* the sales forces of the two companies.

VALERIE: By *pooling* our *resources*, we should create an outstanding team.

STEVE: The problem is *redundancy*. Too many sales personnel are covering the same territory.

VALERIE: I suppose there will be a *gradual* downsizing of personnel until we reduce the number of staff to an appropriate, efficient level.

Short Talk:

In theory, the concept of a merger is a *mutually* agreed combination of *resources* to form one joint company. In reality, a *merger* is more of an *acquisition*, with one company *absorbing* the personnel of another into its existing *infrastructure*. Usually one company has much greater resources and needs another company's strengths to fill in some area. *Redundant* personnel is a potential problem, and employees worry about being downsized when mergers occur.

Fill in the blanks to complete the sentences:

16. Both parties have agreed to the issues and have reached a _____ beneficial settlement.

17. By _____ our resources, we will double our capacity to service customers.

18. With this latest _____, ComSci owns two-thirds of the communications companies doing business on the West Coast.

19. The transportation _____, including the roads, ports, and airports, must be improved if trade is to increase.

20. With the _____, the companies had to decide on a new name which would reflect the joining of the companies.

21. If two employees are doing the same job, chances are their tasks are _____.

22. Because we have limited _____, we have to be cautious of what we spend.

23. We'll _____ the new staff into our already existing structure instead of creating new positions.

24. The staff works well together and has formed a _____ bond over the years.

25. Although no one can confirm it, there's a _____ going around that the company is going out of business.

26. _____ the cost of the new equipment is not something we can do with our limited budget.

27. We need to _____ all of our individual attempts into one unified effort.

28. _____, companies should protect their employees' jobs in a merger, but that doesn't always happen.

29. Changes will be _____ so that employees can adjust to them one at a time.

30. We agree on the _____ but not on the specifics of how we will turn the plan into a reality.

Answer Key

1. an unconfirmed report
2. done or felt by each of the parties involved
3. a grouping of several companies into one
4. basic installations and facilities
5. to take in; to incorporate
6. sticking together
7. unnecessary or excessive
8. wealth, assets
9. to group resources, etcetera, for some common purpose
10. to make or become whole or complete
11. to join into one
12. what should be correct according to some rule or principle
13. gain
14. taking place little by little
15. an idea; a general notion
16. mutually
17. pooling
18. acquisition
19. infrastructure
20. merger
21. redundant
22. resources
23. integrate
24. cohesive
25. rumor
26. absorbing
27. combine
28. in theory
29. gradual
30. concept

20 Negotiations

Match each word or phrase to its meaning:

1. to be convinced   to succeed in affecting or influencing
2. offer   continuing in the face of opposition
3. one-sided   to consult together
4. persistent   something presented for acceptance
5. to take into account   to plead with
6. eager   state of mind in which things are done or given readily or cheerfully
7. to cave in   something one intends to get or do; aim
8. willingness   a point under dispute
9. to reach (an understanding)   to give in to
10. preliminary   having or involving only one side; unfair
11. issue   to consider
12. to confer   to feel sure
13. fair play   honorable treatment, action, or conduct
14. purpose   leading up to the main action
15. to urge   keenly desiring; impatient

Can you figure out the meaning of the italicized words in the following passages?

Conversation One:

LUCY: How can we *reach* an agreement when they won't compromise on a single *issue*?

WARREN: You have to find some way to appeal to their sense of *fair play*. The negotiations can't all be *one-sided*.

LUCY: They're *convinced* we will give in on every point, so they are just waiting for us to *cave in*.

Conversation Two:

WARREN: When you are negotiating, you have to be *persistent*. You can't let the other party think you are disinterested.

LUCY: On the other hand, if you seem too *eager*, they may think you are likely to compromise too much.

WARREN: If there's not a *willingness* on both sides to reach an agreement, then there really is no negotiation.

LUCY: Exactly—both *parties* must feel they've *achieved* their *purpose* or the agreement will not last.

Small Talk:

You have the terms of our *offer* in front of you. These terms *take into account* your *preliminary offer*. We *urge* you to take our *offer* back to your board of directors and *confer* with your accountants. You'll find that our terms are reasonable and, I must add, nonnegotiable.

Fill in the blanks to complete the sentences:

16. When you are unsure of your rights, it's wise to _____ with a specialist.

17. We will have achieved our _____ if we leave this room with a contract in hand.

18. She never takes into account what I've said; our conversations are totally _____.

19. She was _____ and kept asking the same question until she got the answer she wanted.

20. I _____ you to reconsider and accept my offer.

21. The employee was so _____ to resolve the dispute with his boss, he'd agree to just about anything.

22. Before an offer is made, it's good to have a _____ understanding of what the seller wants to receive.

23. We appreciate your _____ to help us and represent our interests in the negotiations.

24. Is there one particular _____ they disagree with or do they not agree with the terms in general?

25. Most of the negotiators claim there was _____, but those representing the smaller countries have said they weren't treated as equals.

26. Are you absolutely _____ that there is nothing more we can do to help you come to a different decision?

27. I'm sure we can _____ an understanding and come up with a solution that works for everyone.

28. We knew she'd _____ when she realized this was the best offer she was going to get.

29. The buyers made the sellers an _____ on the house.

30. Before you agree to the terms, _____ the fact that you may have to relocate.

Answer Key

1. to feel sure
2. something presented for acceptance
3. having or involving only one side; unfair
4. continuing in the face of opposition
5. to consider
6. keenly desiring; impatient
7. to give in to
8. state of mind in which things are done or given readily or cheerfully
9. to succeed in affecting or influencing
10. leading up to the main action
11. a point under dispute
12. to consult together
13. honorable treatment, action, or conduct
14. something one intends to get or do; aim
15. to plead with

16. confer
17. purpose
18. one-sided
19. persistent
20. urge
21. eager
22. preliminary
23. willingness
24. issue
25. fair play
26. convinced
27. reach
28. cave in
29. offer
30. take into account

21 | Office Procedures

Match each word or phrase to its meaning:

1. to take on (an employee) — not having enough workers

2. to collate — producing the desired result with minimum effort, expense or waste

3. consistent — managing daily office affairs

4. to restructure — to entrust to others to do

5. administrative — only lasting for a while, not permanent

6. to put on the back burner — to try to do

7. efficient — holding to the same principles or practice

8. time-consuming — consisting of various kinds or qualities

9. short-handed — to hire

10. miscellaneous — taking much time

11. temporary — to plan or provide a new structure or organization for

12. to delegate — to set apart for a specific purpose

13. to allocate — to deal with later

14. in an effort to — to reduce the size and expenses of operations, mostly by reducing staff

15. to downsize — to put papers in proper order

Can you figure out the meaning of the italicized words in the following passages?

Conversation One:

JEANETTE: I'm *taking on* a part-time employee to help me with my *time-consuming administrative* work.

DAN: Hopefully you'll find someone who's *efficient* and can handle the copying, *collating*, and filing.

JEANETTE: So many things have been *put on the back burner* because I just haven't had the time to get to them.

Conversation Two:

DAN: *In an effort to* get my office in shape, I've asked the finance department to *allocate* money in my budget for *temporary* staff who can come in for a few hours a week to do *miscellaneous* tasks.

JEANETTE: You've been so *short-handed* since the *downsizing*.

DAN: The staff went from 150 to 70 in the *restructuring*. I feel bad for all those people who lost their jobs.

Short Talk:

We need to put together packages for the conference registrants. Here are the materials to be included in the folders. We need to make copies of the materials, *collate* the materials to be in the same order, and place the collated copies in the folders. Each folder should be *consistent* with the other, with the same information in the same order as the others. You can *delegate* specific tasks to the staff members helping you with this project so everyone will have something to do and you'll get done faster.

Fill in the blanks to complete the sentences:

16. Once pages one through ten of the document are copied, _____ them in numerical order so each person gets a full copy.

17. Businesses often hire _____ staff who work only in times of need.

18. Projects that are not time-sensitive will have to be _____ _____ until we have more time to deal with them.

19. When sales tripled, the company had _____ additional staff to meet the customers' demands.

20. More than half of the staff was _____, leaving the company a much smaller operation.

21. If you _____ the work to your staff and assign them each a part of the project, you'll get done much faster.

22. _____ increase internal communications, we'll have staff meetings once a month.

23. I apologize for the delay. My colleague is out of the office today, so we're _____.

24. This paperwork is so _____ that I can't get anything else done.

25. In order to function more efficiently, the firm will _____ its operations and change the way it handles its affairs.

26. _____ assistants manage the daily operations of the office and support the staff.

27. Try to be _____ when you respond to requests so we know that all customers are getting the same information.

28. Her assistant is so _____ that when you ask her for information, you get it right away.

29. The file labeled _____ contains a variety of reports that don't fit into any of the other categories.

30. We must _____ a portion of our budget to buy new office equipment.

Answer Key

1. to hire

2. to put papers in proper order

3. holding to the same principles or practice

4. to plan or provide a new structure or organization for

5. managing daily office affairs

6. to deal with later

7. producing the desired result with minimum effort, expense, or waste

8. taking much time

9. not having enough workers

10. consisting of various kinds or qualities

11. only lasting for a while, not permanent

12. to entrust to others to do

13. to set apart for a specific purpose

14. to try to do

15. to reduce the size and expenses of operations, mostly by reducing staff

16. collate

17. temporary

18. put on the back burner

19. to take on

20. downsized

21. delegate

22. in an effort to

23. short-handed

24. time-consuming

25. restructure

26. administrative

27. consistent

28. efficient

29. miscellaneous

30. allocate

Match each word or phrase to its meaning:

1. evaluation	guide or reference book
2. to come up	to pay back
3. petty cash	lateness
4. tardiness	more likely than not
5. manual	dedication; loyalty
6. principle	instructions in particular routines at workplace, etcetera
7. in all likelihood	profession or occupation
8. to reimburse	to approach
9. career	to review
10. expected	a cash fund for miscellaneous items
11. commitment	explaining itself; obvious
12. to go over	introductory instruction concerning a new situation
13. self-explanatory	judgment of the worth of
14. training	likely to occur or appear
15. orientation	rule of conduct

Can you figure out the meaning of the italicized words in the following passages?

Conversation One:

RON: I was asked to purchase coffee for the office. Will the company pay me back me for that?

LINDA: Yes. The office manager can *reimburse* you from *petty cash*.

RON: Thanks. It's not that much money, but it's the *principle* of the matter. I wouldn't want to be *expected* to supply the office with coffee on a regular basis.

Conversation Two:

LINDA: Your performance *evaluation* is *coming up* next week. How do you think you'll do?

RON: I've worked hard and often stay at the office until late at night. I'm just a little worried because of my recent *tardiness*.

LINDA: *In all likelihood,* you'll probably get a good raise based on your overall *commitment* to the company.

RON: I sure hope so—this job is important to my *career*.

Short Talk:

Follow along with me in your employee *manual* as I *go over* some of the policies and procedures. You'll have a new employee *orientation* later in the week, but I wanted to give you a brief overview of the basics. All employees will receive departmental *training*, which will help you learn about how your department works and your role within the department. The benefits we offer are pretty *self-explanatory.*

Fill in the blanks to complete the sentences:

16. The instructions are _____ and easy to understand once you read them.

17. His _____ to his work is demonstrated by the long hours he keeps.

18. An _____ is planned to make employees feel comfortable in their new work environment.

19. _____, even if I try to save, I will never have enough money to buy that house.

20. We'll review your performance in your written _____.

21. In _____ I agree with your argument, but you don't seem to have the details to back it up.

22. Are new employees _____ to attend the staff meeting?

23. _____ will not be tolerated; employees are expected to arrive on time.

24. The company will _____ employees for all expenses related to their work.

25. Let's _____ the plan one more time so we know we're on the same page.

26. The holidays are _____ and I can't wait for a long vacation.

27. Refer to the _____ when you have questions or need clarification about personnel policies.

28. After she retired, she started a _____ in real estate.

29. _____ is an important function of the human resources office because employees who are not properly trained are not usually efficient.

30. We always have _____ on hand if you need a small sum of money for taxi fare, copies, or other miscellaneous expenses.

Answer Key

1. judgment of the worth of
2. to approach
3. a cash fund for miscellaneous items
4. lateness
5. guide or reference book
6. rule of conduct
7. more likely than not
8. to pay back
9. profession or occupation
10. likely to occur or appear
11. dedication; loyalty
12. to review
13. explaining itself; obvious
14. instruction in particular routines at workplace, etcetera
15. introductory instruction concerning a new situation
16. self-explanatory
17. commitment
18. orientation
19. in all likelihood
20. evaluation
21. principle
22. expected
23. tardiness
24. reimburse
25. go over
26. coming up
27. manual
28. career
29. training
30. petty cash

23 Product Development

Match each word or phrase to its meaning:

1. innovative — the only one of its kind
2. to turn out — introducing something new
3. obsolete — within or utilizing an organization's own staff
4. flexible — designed to be thrown away after a single use
5. in-house — special skill or knowledge
6. unique — to ask for help
7. to call in — working with others
8. technology — outmoded; too old to be used
9. collaboration — adaptable to change
10. expertise — faintly; slightly
11. to build up — to redo plans to change the product
12. disposable — qualifications
13. subtly — to strengthen and develop
14. to redesign — to produce
15. capabilities — the practical application of knowledge

Can you figure out the meaning of the italicized words in the following passages?

Conversation One:

KRISTIN: If we're going to develop a new product line in a timely manner, we'll need to *collaborate* with all concerned departments.

JEROME: We don't have enough *in-house expertise*. We'll have to *call in* outside consultants.

KRISTIN: We need to *build up* our own *capabilities*, so call the head-hunter and give her the okay to begin a recruitment campaign.

Conversation Two:

JEROME: Our competitor's rechargeable batteries are hardly *innovative*. How can they be so popular?

KRISTIN: They're cheaper, for one thing, and their advertising is very effective.

JEROME: We'll have to concentrate our efforts on developing a truly *unique* battery, a battery that never dies.

KRISTIN: Now that would be innovative!

Short Talk:

Our product line needs to be diversified. We cannot depend on the past success of our *disposable* razor. We need to concentrate on developing different kinds of razors for different purposes. If we don't, we'll find our razors *obsolete* and ourselves out of work. Recent improvements in manufacturing *technology* will allow us more *flexibility* in design. By *subtly redesigning* our existing razor we can *turn out* a *disposable* razor for all ages, both sexes, and for any body part.

Fill in the blanks to complete the sentences:

16. With the recent hire of the Asian specialists, we've greatly expanded the firm's _____.

17. Her hints were so _____ that I almost didn't pick up on them.

18. Consumers enjoy new and _____ products that make their lives easier.

19. We need top-level support if we are to get money to fund the development of this product, so _____ all your favors.

20. _____ contact lenses are easy to take care of because you wear them once and then throw them away.

21. Our company prides itself on its _____, which allows us to perform a variety of services for our client.

22. Once we _____ our cash reserves, we'll be in a better position to hire additional staff.

23. We have the staff we need to produce the publications _____ instead of having to hire an outside vendor.

24. Handmade jewelry is _____ because no two pieces are exactly alike.

25. Computers become _____ when they can no longer meet our needs.

26. Working together in _____ with the marketing team has proven to be quite beneficial.

27. His _____ is in advertising; he's very experienced in it.

28. We're going to _____ the packaging so it's more appealing to consumers.

29. _____ has come a long way—from typewriters to computers.

30. If we use the full capacity of the factory, we can _____ hundreds of pairs of sunglasses a day.

Answer Key

1. introducing something new
2. to produce
3. outmoded; too old to be used
4. adaptable to change
5. within or utilizing an organization's own staff
6. the only one of its kind
7. to ask for help
8. the practical application of knowledge
9. working with others
10. special skill or knowledge
11. to strengthen and develop
12. designed to be thrown away after a single use
13. faintly; slightly
14. to redo plans to change the product
15. qualifications
16. capabilities
17. subtle
18. innovative
19. call in
20. disposable
21. flexibility
22. build up
23. in-house
24. unique
25. obsolete
26. collaboration
27. expertise
28. redesign
29. technology
30. turn out

Match each word or phrase to its meaning:

1.	demonstrated	learning news from others
2.	responsibilities	to meet and get to know people who could be helpful
3.	candidate	a good chance; a favorable circumstance
4.	competitive	one seeking a position or office
5.	word of mouth	energetic
6	profession	someone who can work well with others
7.	opportunity	occurring at the same time
8.	in the know	competent in many things
9.	team player	light conversation about common, everyday things; chitchat
10.	to network	proven
11.	dynamic	to search for employment
12.	simultaneously	knowledgeable
13.	to job hunt	occupation
14.	small talk	surpassing or rivaling others
15.	versatile	obligations or duties

Can you figure out the meaning of the italicized words in the following passages?

Conversation One:

FLORENCE: The World Net Corporation is hosting a recruitment reception tonight.

BART: That sounds like a great *opportunity* to *network* and meet people in the *profession*.

FLORENCE: And, since most of the senior level positions aren't advertised, but spread by *word of mouth*, this is a chance to get to know people who are *in the know*, and have access to that information.

Conversation Two:

FLORENCE: *Job hunting* can be a full-time job in itself.

BART: Looking for a job can be challenging. Luckily, you're *versatile* and good at making *small talk*.

FLORENCE: You're right. I started a conversation with a woman about her book and as we talked, she told me about a job opening in her company.

Short Talk:

SPI Incorporated, a *dynamic* communications firm, is seeking a seasoned project manager with *demonstrated* leadership experience. The successful *candidate* will have a college degree or five years of relevant experience, be able to handle multiple tasks *simultaneously*, and be a *team player*. *Responsibilities* include assisting in the development of corporate communications strategies, designing marketing materials, and putting together our production schedule. We offer a *competitive* salary and excellent benefits.

Fill in the blanks to complete the sentences:

16. Working well with others and being a _____ is important to the company's success.

17. Her commitment to the firm is _____ by the countless hours she works.

18. An _____ to meet with CEO's from all the major software companies comes once in a lifetime.

19. When conversations come to a lull, you can always talk about the weather or make some other _____.

20. He wasn't the best _____ that applied for the position because he didn't have the interpersonal skills necessary to deal with customers.

21. Joining business associations that hold _____ events is a great way meet new people with similar interests.

22. Employers seek employees who are _____ and able to handle almost any task.

23. I'm working on two projects _____; I work on one during the morning and on the other during the afternoon.

24. We offer a _____ salary, which equals or surpasses what other companies are paying their employees.

25. Additional _____ will be assigned to you as you master your current duties.

26. There are many books available on _____ because looking for a job can be difficult.

27. Those in the legal _____ often complain about long hours and heavy workloads.

28. The job wasn't advertised; I learned about it through _____ _____ from a friend who works for the company.

29. He's a _____ individual, full of life and energy.

30. Talking with people _____ can be beneficial because they have access to information you might not otherwise get.

Answer Key

1. proven
2. obligations or duties
3. one seeking a position or office
4. surpassing or rivaling others
5. learning news from others
6. occupation
7. a good chance; a favorable circumstance
8. knowledgeable
9. someone who can work well with others
10. to meet and get to know people who could be helpful
11. energetic
12. occurring at the same time
13. to search for employment
14. light conversation about common, everyday things; chitchat
15. competent in many things
16. team player
17. demonstrated
18. opportunity
19. small talk
20. candidate
21. networking
22. versatile
23. simultaneously
24. competitive
25. responsibilities
26. job hunting
27. profession
28. word of mouth
29. dynamic
30. in the know

Match each word or phrase to its meaning:

1. accurate	following from
2. to malfunction	not current
3. elaborate	process to ensure products are well made
4. to gather	to collect
5. utility	to bring into proper order
6. standard	developed in considerable detail; complicated
7. as a result of	determination to act in a specified way
8. assurance	careful and exact; free from errors
9. outdated	something established for use as a rule or basis of comparison in measuring value, quality, quantity, etcetera
10. consumer	the outcome
11. to coordinate	proof
12. intention	usefulness
13. quality control	confidence
14. evidence	to fail to work as it should
15. result	person that uses goods and services

Can you figure out the meaning of the italicized words in the following passages?

Conversation One:

MARTY: By the time we finish the exhaustive testing required by the government, our product will be *outdated.*

DOLORES: We've *gathered* the *evidence* required. I think we should submit the data for approval.

MARTY: We have to *coordinate* the release of the information with the public relations department, who will decide when to announce our *results.*

Conversation Two:

MARTY: This is the most *elaborate* procedure I've ever seen.

DOLORES: Our *quality control* tests are very strict. The appliance can't *malfunction* in a *consumer's* hands.

MARTY: Yes, you wouldn't want to risk a lawsuit.

DOLORES: We *intend* to minimize potential problems and maximize product utility.

Short Talk:

We want to congratulate the director of the Research Department and her colleagues for developing the HumidoGraph, which will be, if I may brag, the most *accurate* measurement tool for reading humidity levels available on the market. *As a result of* the *elaborate* testing and exhaustive studies performed by the department, we can say with *assurance* that this product will set the *standard* for instruments recording humidity levels.

Fill in the blanks to complete the sentences:

16. I've _____ the data on the housing industry and will now collect the other information you requested.

17. Our _____ policy lets customers know they can have confidence in our products.

18. Every product is checked by inspectors as part of our _____ efforts.

19. It is our _____ to provide accurate reports.

20. Since the equipment would not function, we questioned the _____ of continuing the experiment.

21. Our goal is to make _____ feel good about what they buy.

22. We've gone over the report very carefully so you can be sure the information contained within it is _____.

23. _____ the complaints we've received from our customers, we're redesigning the product.

24. The _____ of the research indicate that market demand for the product will continue to grow.

25. Cheaply made products tend to _____ and have to be repaired or replaced often.

26. The procedures for registering for the license are so _____ that I had to read over them three times before I understood what to do.

27. The public relations department will _____ the details for the press conference.

28. Can you provide _____, such as facts and figures, to support your thesis?

29. The information contained in this ten-year old publication must be _____.

30. When compared against the other products on the market, this one is clearly below _____.

Answer Key

1. careful and exact; free from errors
2. to fail to work as it should
3. developed in considerable detail; complicated
4. to collect
5. usefulness
6. something established for use as a rule or basis of comparison in measuring value, quality, quantity, etcetera
7. following from
8. confidence
9. not current
10. person that uses goods and services
11. to bring into proper order
12. determination to act in a specified way
13. process to ensure products are well made
14. proof
15. the outcome

16. gathered
17. assurance
18. quality control
19. intention
20. utility
21. consumers
22. accurate
23. as a result of
24. results
25. malfunction
26. elaborate
27. coordinate
28. evidence
29. outdated
30. standard

26 Salaries

Match each word or phrase to its meaning:

1. promotion — yearly recurrence of a date of a past event

2. to be entitled to — to have the right to something

3. retroactive — to stop working to relax, usually because of age

4. anniversary — programs offered to employees as a complement to their earnings

5. earnings — increase in pay

6. raise — payment over and above what is due

7. to retire — something extra for good work

8. pension — full of initiative and energy

9. benefits — payment for services

10. modest — advancement in position

11. bonus — the way one carries out work

12. reward — not too large in amount

13. performance — a fixed amount paid to a retired employee

14. enterprising — money earned

15. compensation — effective as of a past date

Can you figure out the meaning of the italicized words in the following passages?

Conversation One:

TARA: Did you hear that Sally just got a *promotion* and *raise*, which is *retroactive* to June?

MALCOLM: Yes. The announcement was sent to everyone through interoffice e-mail. Her *earnings* must be well into the six digits now.

TARA: I'm really happy for her because she has an *enterprising* spirit and works hard. This will be her tenth *anniversary* with the company.

Conversation Two:

MALCOLM: Mary is going to *retire* next month. Can you believe she's been with the company for 45 years?

TARA: That sure is a long time. Beats me by a long shot.

MALCOLM: I'm sure she'll be rewarded for her time with the company with a good *pension* plan.

TARA: Yes, especially since the company makes monthly contributions and matches any individual contributions made to the pension plan.

Short Talk:

Welcome to the Travel Company. I want to talk with you about your *benefits*. We offer a *modest* salary, which is complemented by a generous *bonus* at the end of each year. *Rewards* are also given for outstanding *performance*. As a full-time employee, you are also *entitled* to full health coverage. Our employees are quite pleased with their total *compensation* package.

Fill in the blanks to complete the sentences:

16. The company offers _____ to employees who get high marks for customer service.

17. After two years of service, you will be eligible to enroll in our _____ plan, which will be paid out to you upon retirement.

18. My supervisor gave me a holiday _____. Now I have extra money to go shopping with.

19. Each employee is _____ to certain basic benefits that include health and life insurance.

20. Your _____ package includes your annual salary, benefits, and an annual bonus.

21. Your year-to-date _____ can be found on your pay stub, which lists a running total of the amounts of each paycheck.

22. He was reprimanded for his poor _____ after failing to complete a number of projects on time.

23. Because your performance review was held after your anniversary date, your salary increase will be _____ to the actual anniversary date.

24. I got a _____ from $10 an hour to $15 an hour.

25. My employer offers great _____ like a month of paid vacation, ten paid personal days, and free membership to a gym.

26. Based on his outstanding performance and dedication to his work, Jim has been _____ from manager to vice president.

27. Successful businesses are built on the energy and initiative of _____ employees.

28. I don't mind getting a _____ salary because it's the pleasure of the work and not the money that's important.

29. My dream is to _____ early in life so I have more time to do the things I enjoy, without the pressure of a career.

30. Tomorrow marks my third _____ with the agency. Can you believe I've been here three years already?

Answer Key

1. advancement in position
2. to have the right to something
3. effective as of a past date
4. yearly recurrence of a date of a past event
5. money earned
6. increase in pay
7. to stop working to relax, usually because of age
8. a fixed amount paid to a retired employee
9. programs offered to employees as a complement to their earnings
10. not too large in amount
11. payment over and above what is due
12. something extra for good work
13. the way one carries out work
14. full of initiative and energy
15. payment for services
16. rewards
17. pension
18. bonus
19. entitled
20. compensation
21. earnings
22. performance
23. retroactive
24. raise
25. benefits
26. promoted
27. enterprising
28. modest
29. retire
30. anniversary

27 Sales

Match each word or phrase to its meaning:

1. associate	a placard bearing information, advertising, etcetera
2. display	ruling; prevailing
3. discount	colleague
4. outlet	a reduction from the usual price
5. to afford	a percentage of money from sales
6. sign	to learn by example
7. commission	the sale of goods directly to the customer
8. retail	too attractive to withstand
9. brand name	to be aware
10. dominant	to look for similarities and differences between two or more things
11. to take notice	a market for goods
12. to pick up on	any methods to gain an end
13. to compare	to be able to buy without spending too much
14. tactics	exhibition
15. irresistible	the name by which a certain label is known

Can you figure out the meaning of the italicized words in the following passages?

Conversation One:

KATE: Working in *retail* is fun. You get to meet people and make *commission* on each item you sell.

SYLVESTER: I've been a sales *associate* for years, and I still enjoy working here. The employee *discounts* are what I like best.

KATE: I bought an entire outfit last week for next to nothing. It was on sale, and I got an additional 20 percent off with the employee *discount*.

Conversation Two:

SYLVESTER: The ceramic *display* should be placed in a *dominant* location because we need to move this merchandise.

KATE: Once it's assembled, I'll make sure there are adequate *signs* so customers will *take notice* of it.

SYLVESTER: I'm glad you're *picking up* on the sales *tactics*.

KATE: You bet. I'll soon know all the tricks of the trade.

Short Talk:

Visit our *outlet* stores where you can save up to 50 percent on all *brand names*. You'll find the most popular designer fashions at prices you can *afford*. *Compare* our prices with the leading shops, and you'll find the savings *irresistible*. Our prices will bring you out to the outlet and our wide selection will keep you there.

Fill in the blanks to complete the sentences:

16. The _____ indicate where customers can easily find the items on sale.

17. _____ stores buy their wares from the manufacturers and sell them to directly to the customer.

18. _____ stores have lower prices because they have less overhead than other retail stores.

19. Placing candy near the checkout counter is one of the sales _____ stores use to get customers to buy more.

20. If you _____ prices before you buy expensive items, you can save lot of money.

21. I've got to have this dress; it's _____.

22. She wears only _____, and all her clothes must carry the label of well-known designers.

23. Our product display will make people stand up and _____ of the fine products we sell.

24. I can't _____ to buy new furniture unless I give up eating for a month to save money.

25. The sales _____ was very helpful in finding me the perfect suit for my interview.

26. The color red is more _____ than white, so let's put the red shirts in front to attract more attention.

27. Sales persons receive _____ on every sale they make.

28. Many stores offer significant _____ during the holidays and you can save a bundle.

29. Once you're here for a while, you'll start _____ how things work.

30. We've sold out of that item; the only one left is the _____ model.

Answer Key

1. colleague
2. exhibition
3. a reduction from the usual price
4. a market for goods
5. to be able to buy without spending too much
6. a placard bearing information, advertising, etcetera
7. a percentage of money from sales
8. the sale of goods directly to the customer
9. the name by which a certain label is known
10. ruling; prevailing
11. to be aware
12. to learn by example
13. to look for similarities and differences between two or more things
14. any methods to gain an end
15. too attractive to withstand
16. signs
17. retail
18. outlet
19. tactics
20. compare
21. irresistible
22. brand names
23. take notice
24. afford
25. associate
26. dominant
27. commission
28. discounts
29. picking up on
30. display

28 Shipping

Match each word or phrase to its meaning:

1. journal — obtainment

2. backlogged — city with a harbor where boats go to unload cargo

3. fleet — to know where something is

4. port — to move goods from one place to another

5. supplier — group of ships or trucks

6. requisition — person who provides or sells the goods

7. batch — load carried by ships or trucks

8. procurement — behind schedule

9. cargo — maker of goods

10. warehouse — book with entries of orders

11. to keep track of — the actual goods shipped

12. shipment — a secondary contract for part or all of the work to be performed under the contract

13. manufacturer — one group of goods

14. to transport — building in which goods are kept; storage facility

15. subcontract — formal written order

Can you figure out the meaning of the italicized words in the following passages?

Conversation One:

HECTOR: I placed an order for a *batch* of lumber that we have still not received.

MARIANA: That *shipment* was expected to come in last week, but has been delayed. One of the *cargo* trucks in our *fleet* broke down, which has put us behind schedule. All orders are now *backlogged*.

HECTOR: Looks like I might have to find another *supplier*.

Conversation Two:

MARIANA: Have you seen the *journal* of *requisitions*? I need to check on an order.

HECTOR: No. You might want to check with the *warehouse*. The supervisor should have a copy.

MARIANA: I don't have time to look all over for it. What good is having a journal to track orders if you can't *keep track* of it?

Short Talk:

Our recent *procurement* of new ships will allow us to move *cargo* faster and meet the growing needs of our customers. We'll be responsible for picking up cars from the *manufacturers* in Japan and *transporting* them to car dealerships throughout the United States. This is a big job, so we'll need help. We'll *subcontract* local companies to transport the cars from our main *ports* to the dealerships. We'll also expand the storage facilities at the ports so we'll have someplace to put the cars while they're waiting to be picked up.

Fill in the blanks to complete the sentences:

16. Your job is _____ shipments so when customers call to check on their orders, you will be able to tell them exactly where they are.

17. Since we don't have enough drivers, we'll have to _____ with another company to help us fulfill the orders.

18. Report any problems with the equipment to its _____.

19. Our _____ of trucks is well maintained and has an outstanding track record for reliability.

20. The _____ office handles the purchases of large equipment.

21. The furniture won't fit in my car. I'll need to rent a van to _____ it from the store to my home.

22. This _____ of cars is only part of the total shipment.

23. Our _____ called to say she has the materials you ordered ready for pickup.

24. We have too many requests for supplies and not enough hours in the day to fill them. All orders are totally _____.

25. Once the _____ is loaded on to the truck, it will be driven to its final destination.

26. Luckily, the damaged _____, which consisted of glassware from Europe, was insured.

27. I'll check the _____ to see if we have that item in stock.

28. Record each order in the _____ so we have an up-to-date account of our business transactions.

29. Every customer must submit a written _____ for supplies. Phone orders will no longer be taken.

30. The _____ is bustling with the activity of ships being loaded and unloaded.

Answer Key

1. book with entries of orders
2. behind schedule
3. group of ships or trucks
4. city with a harbor where boats go to unload cargo
5. person who provides or sells the goods
6. formal written order
7. one group of goods
8. obtainment
9. load carried by ships or trucks
10. building where goods are kept; storage facility
11. to know where something is
12. the actual goods shipped
13. maker of goods
14. to move goods from one place to another
15. a secondary contract for part or all of the work to be performed under the contract

16. to keep track of
17. subcontract
18. manufacturer
19. fleet
20. procurement
21. transport
22. batch
23. supplier
24. backlogged
25. cargo
26. shipment
27. warehouse
28. journal
29. requisition
30. port

29 Taxes

Match each word or phrase to its meaning:

1. to itemize — to get money back
2. deductions — total income before taxes are taken out
3. to refund — to go over
4. penalty — relative you can claim you support
5. to calculate — to collect taxes from the source
6. gross income — level of taxes you pay
7. tax bracket — form for filing taxes
8. liable — freedom from obligation
9. to withhold — sum of money imposed for violations
10. tax return — to list separately
11. to review — marital position
12. dependent — money received from keeping money in the bank
13. filing status — legally responsible
14. interest income — to figure out by using math
15. exemption — subtractions

Can you figure out the meaning of the italicized words in the following passages?

Conversation One:

BARRY: Since you now own a home, if you *itemize deductions*, you'll get a larger *refund*.

ALEXANDRA: I hope so. Last year I had to pay a *penalty* for not paying enough taxes.

Conversation Two:

ALEXANDRA: I've started to *calculate* my taxes, and boy, am I confused! What does *gross income* mean?

BARRY: Gross income is the total of all the money paid to you by your employer.

ALEXANDRA: Thanks to my raise, my salary has gone up enough to put me into a higher *tax bracket*.

BARRY: You should have more money *deducted* from each paycheck. If your employer increases the amount *withheld* from your paycheck, you won't have to pay so much at the end of the tax year.

Short Talk:

Please have your *tax return* in front of you so we can *go over* your questions. Please refer to the instructions on the first page of the tax booklet to see if you can claim an *exemption* from filing. If you had a tax *liability* last year, chances are you will have to file and pay taxes again this year. Are you married or single? Your *filing status* will reflect your situation. Any family members living with you may be claimed as *dependents* if certain criteria are met. Don't forget to list your *interest income*, which you will see on your year-end bank statement.

Fill in the blanks to complete the sentences:

16. You can take an exemption for each _____, including a relative or someone you supported during the tax year.

17. After you _____ your taxes, make sure to check your math.

18. Your wages, interest from your savings account, plus any other income make up your _____.

19. If you are single, your tax _____ is one, assuming you can't claim any other deductions.

20. Withholding tax is the money _____ from your paychecks for taxes paid directly from your employer to the government.

21. The higher your salary, the higher the _____, and the more you pay in taxes.

22. Complete your _____ and mail these forms to the Internal Revenue Service by April 15.

23. Will you _____ my calculations to make sure they're right?

24. This year, I have many deductions, so I'll _____ each deduction I can make from my taxable income.

25. I paid $12,000 in taxes this year and my accountant told me I only had to pay $7,000. Looks like I'll be getting a big _____.

26. My savings account has increased with the interest from the bank, but now I'll have to pay taxes on this _____.

27. You can claim an _____ if you did not have to pay taxes last year and do not expect to have tax liability this year.

28. Mortgage interest, state and local taxes, and charitable contributions can be claimed as _____.

29. If you don't have enough taxes withheld from your check during the year, you might face a _____ on the amount underpaid at the end of that year.

30. Each American citizen who reaches a certain income level has a tax _____ and is responsible for paying taxes.

Answer Key

1. to list separately
2. subtractions
3. to get money back
4. sum of money imposed for violations
5. to figure out by using math
6. total income before taxes are taken out
7. level of taxes you pay
8. legally responsible
9. to collect taxes from the source
10. form for filing taxes
11. to go over
12. relative you can claim you support
13. marital position
14. money received from keeping money in the bank
15. freedom from obligation
16. dependent
17. calculate
18. gross income
19. filing status
20. withheld
21. tax bracket
22. tax return
23. review
24. itemize
25. refund
26. interest income
27. exemption
28. deductions
29. penalty
30. liability

30 | Telephone

Match each word or phrase to its meaning:

1. directory	computerized system that answers the phone and allows callers to record messages
2. operator	phone call with three or more people
3. area code	person who answers the phone
4. to take a call	do not interrupt; leave alone
5. to disconnect	list of telephone numbers
6. to transfer	calling back and forth; being unable to reach the person you are calling
7. conference call	to receive a call
8. to put on hold	to disrupt someone in action
9. extension	to make a caller wait
10. voice mail	to forward the call to another person's phone
11. phone tag	to end the call by putting down the phone on the receiver
12. to put down	to lose a connection
13. do not disturb	to write down
14. to hang up	number assigned to individual phones
15. to interrupt	three-digit exchange assigned to geographical areas

Can you figure out the meaning of the italicized words in the following passages?

Conversation One:

AMELIA: Hello, *directory* assistance. May I help you?

GEORGE: Yes, *operator*, I'd like to make a call but don't know the *area code* for Houston.

AMELIA: Here's the area code. *Put this down* for future reference.

Conversation Two:

MR. PAULING: Ms. Adams, you have a call on line one. Shall I *transfer* the call to your *extension*?

MS. ADAMS: I'll *take the call*, but I hope it's quick because I'm expecting a *conference call* with Ms. Manet and Mr. Fujita soon. Please *interrupt* me if they call.

MR. PAULING: Oh, no! He got *disconnected* by mistake when I *put him on hold*.

MS. ADAMS: If he calls back, please *transfer* him to my *voice mail* so he can leave a message.

Short Talk:

Our new phone and *voice mail* system can help you get more done at the office. This system comes with features like "*do not disturb*," which allows you to block phone calls at your desk. No more writing notes or having to take a message from callers. Callers can leave detailed and private messages for you in voice mail, reducing the amount of time you spend playing *phone tag* with your clients and the amount of messages taken by your receptionist. So *hang up* the phone and leave the answering to voice mail.

Fill in the blanks to complete the sentences:

16. Lisa, I have a call for you; I'll _____ it to your phone now.

17. This is HiTech. If you know the _____ of the person you are trying to reach, dial those numbers now.

18. I need to call information in Washington, DC; do you know the _____ for the city?

19. Let me check the telephone _____ for the number you're trying to find.

20. This "_____" feature allows me to concentrate on my work without the disruption of phone calls.

21. If you'd like to make a call, please _____ and try the number again.

22. _____, I need the number for the Cosco Company in Salt Lake City, please.

23. If Ms. Salmon calls, I want _____ because I need to talk with her directly.

24. Please do not _____ me during this important meeting.

25. Because callers can leave detailed messages in my _____, I can get the information without having to call them back.

26. He was on his cellular phone when he called and we got _____ when his phone battery died.

27. Make sure _____; it is an important message that I have to get to Mr. Smith.

28. Let's set up a _____ so we can all discuss this issue together over the phone.

29. I need _____ while I get the other line that's ringing.

30. We've been trying unsuccessfully to reach each other by phone for so long. In order to stop this _____, let's just meet tomorrow at noon.

Answer Key

1. list of telephone numbers
2. person who answers the phone
3. three-digit exchange assigned to geographical areas
4. to receive a call
5. to lose a connection
6. to forward the call to another person's phone
7. phone call with three or more people
8. to make a caller wait
9. number assigned to individual phones
10. computerized system that answers the phone and allows callers to record messages
11. calling back and forth; being unable to reach the person you are calling
12. to write down
13. do not interrupt; leave alone
14. to end the call by putting down the phone on the receiver
15. to disrupt someone in action

16. transfer
17. extension
18. area code
19. directory
20. do not disturb
21. hang up
22. operator
23. to take the call
24. interrupt
25. voice mail
26. disconnected
27. to put this down
28. conference call
29. to put you on hold
30. phone tag

Index

About KAPLAN

Educational Centers

Kaplan Educational Centers is one of the nation's premier education companies, providing individuals with a full range of resources to achieve their educational and career goals. Kaplan, celebrating its 60th anniversary, is a wholly-owned subsidiary of The Washington Post Company.

TEST PREPARATION & ADMISSIONS

Kaplan's nationally-recognized test prep courses cover more than 20 standardized tests, including entrance exams for secondary school, college and graduate school as well as foreign language and professional licensing exams. In addition, Kaplan offers private tutoring and comprehensive, one-to-one admissions and application advice for students applying to graduate school.

SCORE! EDUCATIONAL CENTERS

SCORE! after-school learning centers help students in grades K-8 build academic skills, confidence and goal-setting skills in a motivating, sports-oriented environment. Kids use a cutting-edge, interactive curriculum that continually assesses and adapts to their academic needs and learning style. Enthusiastic Academic Coaches serve as positive role models, creating a high-energy atmosphere where learning is exciting and fun for kids. With nearly 40 centers today, SCORE! continues to open new centers nationwide.

KAPLAN LEARNING SERVICES

Kaplan Learning Services provides customized assessment, education and training programs to K-12 schools, universities and businesses to help students and employees reach their educational and career goals.

KAPLAN INTERNATIONAL

Kaplan serves international students and professionals in the U.S. through Access America, a series of intensive English language programs, and LCP

International Institute, a leading provider of intensive English language programs at on-campus centers in California, Washington and New York. Kaplan and LCP offer specialized services to sponsors including placement at top American universities, fellowship management, academic monitoring and reporting and financial administration.

KAPLOAN

Students can get key information and advice about educational loans for college and graduate school through **KapLoan** (Kaplan Student Loan Information Program). Through an affiliation with one of the nation's largest student loan providers, **KapLoan** helps direct students and their families through the often bewildering financial aid process.

KAPLAN PUBLISHING

Kaplan Books, a joint imprint with Simon & Schuster, publishes books in test preparation, admissions, education,career development and life skills; Kaplan and *Newsweek* jointly publish the highly successful guides, **How to Get Into College** and **How to Choose a Career & Graduate School**. SCORE! and *Newsweek* have teamed up to publish **How to Help Your Child Suceed in School**.

Kaplan InterActive delivers award-winning, high quality educational products and services including Kaplan's best-selling **Higher Score** test-prep software and sites on the internet **(http://www.kaplan.com)** and America Online. Kaplan and Cendant Software are jointly developing, marketing and distributing educational software for the kindergarten through twelfth grade retail and school markets.

KAPLAN CAREER SERVICES

Kaplan helps students and graduates find jobs through Kaplan Career Services, the leading provider of career fairs in North America. The division includes **Crimson & Brown Associates**, the nation's leading diversity recruiting and publishing firm, and **The Lendman Group and Career Expo**, both of which help clients identify highly sought-after technical personnel and sales and marketing professionals.

COMMUNITY OUTREACH

Kaplan provides educational resources to thousands of financially disadvantaged students annually, working closely with educational institutions, not-for-profit groups, government agencies and other grass roots organizations on a variety of national and local support programs. Also, Kaplan centers enrich local communities by employing high school, college and graduate students, creating valuable work experiences for vast numbers of young people each year.